Mary Immaculate
Patroness of Our Country
Pray for Us

My Journey

Musings of a Missionary

My Journey

Musings of a Missionary

Lawrence Sabatini, c.s.

Sabatini, Lawrence.
1930-
My Journey: Musings of a Missionary / Lawrence Sabatini, c.s.
255 p. cm.
Includes index.
ISBN-10 0615346960 – ISBN-13 9780615346960
1. Sabatini, Lawrence
2. Christian missionaries—Canada—British Columbia
I. Title
BV2810 .B7 S2 2010

Photographs contributed by friends, colleagues and family members of Lawrence Sabatini, c.s.
Jacket background photograph by Janice Carapellucci.

Edited by Mary Elizabeth Brown, Ph.D., Staten Island, New York, U.S.A.
Graphic design by Janice Carapellucci, Carapellucci Design, Brooklyn, New York, U.S.A.

This book is typeset in the typeface Dante which was designed by Giovanni Mardersteig, Charles Malin and Matthew Carter in the 1950s for letterpress printing and revised in the 1990s by Monotype's staff for digital use.

Printed by Sheridan Books, Inc., Ann Arbor, Michigan, U.S.A., in 2010.

First edition

Contents

Foreword

PERHAPS it is not so unusual for a person in the sunset years of his life ("golden age"?) to reflect on his life's story, especially if he has the benefit of a diary. My tale does not contain only what some might consider human interest stories. My journey is a reflection on the spiritual dimension of my life as a missionary priest and bishop and how all of this transpired. Throughout these many years I have seen the hand of God working within me in ways I could never have dreamed humanly possible. Thus, above all, my heart is full of gratitude to our gracious God for His immense love for me and all His creatures.

I wish to express my heartfelt gratitude to my parents, who taught us children to be proud to be Americans and to love our Italian heritage; to my siblings, relatives, friends, priests, educators and others who have impacted my life in truly memorable ways. My Scalabrinian family played a huge role in this.

There are other people I must acknowledge gratefully. Without their help and support, this modest work might not have reached fruition. My typist, Gloria Dallmeier, for patiently deciphering my almost illegible handwriting; my editor, Dr. Mary Elizabeth Brown, Scalabrinian archivist and author of several books on migration, for meticulously vetting every page of the manuscript; my designer, Janice Carapellucci, for her important contribution; my confreres, Rev. Ezio Marchetto, c.s. and Rev. René Manenti, c.s., Assistant and Executive Director, respectively, of the Center for Migration Studies in New York City, for walking me through the whole publishing process; Bishop David Monroe of Kamloops, British Columbia, for graciously sending photos of my ministry in the diocese, especially among the aboriginal people; Alberta Catalano for scanning all the photos prior to publication and for taking many of the photos herself; Fr. Aldo Vendramin, c.s. for his photos; Donna Hurwitz for the library cataloguing; and Sheridan Books, Inc. in Ann Arbor, Michigan, for printing the completed work.

This is my story. It is what it is. This written account does not pretend to be in the same class of such great works as *The Story of a Soul* by St. Thérèse of Lisieux, or *The Diary of a Country Priest* by Georges Bernanos, or Blessed Pope John XXIII's *Journal of a Soul,* or even Bill O'Reilly's *Bold Fresh.* Mine is simply a series of random musings of my youth and missionary activities.

Walk with me now on my journey down memory lane.

The Lord
called me before
I was born.

(Isa 49:1)

MY life outside the womb began on May 15, 1930, at 1054 W. Erie Street in the near Northwest side of the city of Chicago. I was the fourth of five children born to Dominic Sabatini and Ada Pioli. I was born at home with the assistance of a neighborhood midwife. Not many hospital births in our neighborhood at that time.

Baptism with sponsors Addolorata and Settimo Cassettari.

I was baptized on June 8, 1930 in the first of three churches named Santa Maria Addolorata on Grand and Peoria. This church burned down three weeks after my baptism. The second church was on May and Erie Streets. This is the church I best remember. I made my first Holy Communion there in May of 1938. I was confirmed on June 4, 1940, by Bishop Bernard Sheil, Auxiliary Bishop of Chicago, at Santa Maria Addolorata. I said my first Solemn Mass in September of 1957 in the same church. Shortly thereafter our church, home, school and entire neighborhood were razed to make way for what is now the Kennedy expressway. Later, the third Santa Maria Addolorata church and school were built on Ada and Ohio Streets where it still stands.

With Fr. Primo and brother Joe in front of the second Santa Maria Addolorata Church on the corner of May and Erie Streets, 1941.

Santa Maria Addolorata was staffed by the Missionary Fathers of St. Charles, also known as Scalabrinians after their founder Blessed John Baptist Scalabrini. This saintly bishop of Piacenza in Italy founded this religious congregation in 1887 in response to the need

First Communion with friends Lee and Syl D'Agostino.

for pastoral ministry to migrants who left their homeland for distant and unfamiliar shores. This community bears the designation "c.s." (Congregation of Scalabrini).

My father (Domingo-Domenico-Dominic) was born of Italian immigrants in Campinas, São Paulo, Brazil. My mother was born in Italy in the very small town of Valbona (Garfagnana) in the Province of Lucca in Tuscany. When my paternal grandparents retired from their menial jobs in the heartlands of Brazil, they returned to Italy taking with them their teenager Domingo. It was there in Valbona that Domingo met Ada and the two were married in the parish church. The economic situation in Italy at the time was extremely poor, especially in the small towns. My parents decided to immigrate to the United States with their first two children: Genoveffa (Jenny) and Italo (Ralph). My brother Giuseppe (Joseph) was the first child born on U.S. soil. He was followed by me (Renzo, later Lorenzo and finally Lawrence). The last of the family was Olga who was born thirteen months after my birth. My mother sometimes facetiously referred to her five children as "le cinque piaghe del Signore" or "the five wounds of the Lord." Actually we weren't that bad, except sometimes.

It was in the year 1924 that my parents arrived in the U.S. via Ellis Island. My parents were among the more than two and one-half million Italians who between the years 1892 and 1921 approached America's doors to freedom and opportunity. Ellis Island was the major port of disembarkation. It closed its doors in 1954 and the brick and limestone buildings gradually deteriorated. During my years in Staten Island, New York, from 1948 to 1951, many times I took the five cent ferry boat ride from St. George to the Battery in Manhattan. During the ride I would lean over the rail of the ferry boat and survey with great interest and emotion that huge, dilapidated structure of Ellis Island. I recalled what my parents told us about their experience there. Here is their story.

Upon arrival, our parents were given numbered tags, which were pinned on their clothes. This reminded me of the Star of David which was sewn on the clothes of Jews during the Holocaust. My parents were among the thousands of people who were ushered into the huge registry hall for processing. When that was completed, they were sent up to the second floor where a group of doctors examined them for signs of any possible disease. Those suspected of having any symptoms would receive chalk marks on their clothes. My father was one of them. He was suspected of having tuberculosis. He faced the prospect of being sent back to Italy. He was placed in quarantine in a special area of the building where he was given various tests. In the meantime, my mother knew nothing of this and her inquiries were fruitless because she could not speak a word of English. She was in a state of panic, having to look after two infant children all by herself. The long voyage across the unfriendly Atlantic with over a thousand passengers of more than twelve different nationalities had already drained her. Besides, the lodging aboard ship was substandard and cases of malnutrition were not uncommon. Finally, after mom's three excruciating days, my father was cleared and reunited with her and the children. They then pursued their journey by train to Chicago.

Confirmation with sponsor Louie the "cyclist".

In 1982, President Ronald Reagan asked Lee Iacocca, Chairman of the Board of Chrysler Corporation of America, to undertake a private-sector fund-raising effort to restore Ellis Island to its original state. As a child of Italian immigrants himself, Iacocca accepted the challenge and was able to raise over 160 million dollars to complete the restoration. On September 10, 1990, Ellis Island was re-opened to the public. I was so proud of this achievement.

I had a great desire to visit the renovated Ellis Island and see for myself what my parents endured there. My wish came true not once but twice in May 1992 and June 2001. I was moved to tears as I retraced the steps of my parents' painful journey: the huge registry hall; the place where the medical exams were conducted; the room where my father was quarantined; the picture of the ship that brought my parents to the U.S.; the original photos of migrants like my parents arriving on the Island with one or two suitcases, the sum total of their worldly possessions; the wall of honor with the names of benefactors such as my oldest sister Jenny who was one of the two infants my parents brought with them from the "old country." As I walked from place to place, the words of the song "America the Beautiful" lingered in my ears. As I visited Liberty Island, I read with emotion the beautiful inscription of Emma Lazarus on the pedestal of the Statue of Liberty. "Give me your tired, your poor, your huddled masses yearning to breathe free, the wretched refuse of your teeming shore, send these, the homeless, tempest tossed to me. I lift my lamp beside the golden door." God bless America!

My infancy was anything but normal. My parents told me that when I was about one and a half years old, I was diagnosed with diphtheria which in the 1930's was life-threatening, especially in children. I was taken to the hospital where I was placed in quarantine for several days. My parents were allowed to see me only through a window in the door. My parents told me that when I would see them in the window, I would get excited and bite my wrist, a habit which I carried with me throughout my early years, not knowing the origin of that gesture until my parents told me. One day, the attending physician informed my anguishing parents that I had no hope of recovery. He suggested that it would be better if they took me home to die rather than pass away in the hospital. As a last desperate effort, my parents bundled me up and took me to the office of a family doctor in our neighborhood. Whatever he did or prescribed in that visit obviously worked. I suppose the good Lord had plans for me.

Blessed Scalabrini proved to be a man of vision. He learned that 11,000 people had left his own diocese for the New World. Some of them wrote back to him deploring the condition in which they were living. They felt alone and abandoned in an environment that was not always very receptive of immigrants. They had no priests to minister to them in their native language or to help them with their material as well as spiritual needs. The pastoral heart of this extraordinary apostle prompted him to travel up and down all of Italy to recruit priests who would be willing to volunteer their service to these immigrants, especially in North and South America for a period of at least five years. His earnest plea touched many hearts and several priests responded. With the permission of their local ordinaries, Bishop Scalabrini sent these missionaries overseas to serve needy families in the United States and Brazil. Bishop Scalabrini did not simply dispatch these early missionaries. With the permission of Pope Leo XIII, he himself made trips to Brazil and the United States to observe the work of his missionaries and their communities and to encourage them in their apostolic endeavors.

Bishop Scalabrini arrived in the U.S. on August 3, 1901. On October 9, after visiting several missions, he was received by President Theodore Roosevelt. The bishop discussed with the President the whole question of immigration and the problems connected with it. The President acknowledged the merits and sacrifices of the Italian immigrants. Scalabrini was very pleased when the President told him that the immigrants are worthy of respect for their willingness to do difficult jobs to survive.

Bishop Scalabrini's pastoral concern for migrants was not limited to Italians. His vision was to help all immigrants and refugees in their struggle for dignity. In fact, in his visit to Boston on September 5, 1901, Bishop Scalabrini visited a Polish mission where he had assigned one of his early Polish missionaries.

Recognizing the importance of lay participation in the ministry to immigrants, Bishop Scalabrini also founded a lay organization called the St. Raphael Society. Its goal was to provide assistance to the migrants in port cities of embarkation and disembarkation.

One of Bishop Scalabrini's missionaries in Brazil was Fr. Giuseppe Marchetti, who founded the Christopher Columbus orphanage in São Paulo. Fr. Marchetti wrote to Bishop Scalabrini indicating the urgent need of founding a congregation of women with the specific aim of aiding the immigrants and caring for the orphans. Bishop Scalabrini agreed. Fr. Marchetti and his sister, Mother Mary Assunta Marchetti, were instructed to begin the process. With the blessing of Bishop Scalabrini, in 1895 the Missionary Sisters of St. Charles were born. Blessed John Baptist Scalabrini truly earned the title of "Father To the Immigrants." Both the Scalabrinian Fathers and Sisters are important parts of my story.

60th anniversary of religious profession of Sr. Anselma (MSCS) Provincial House in Melrose Park, July 2009.

In my many years in the seminary in Chicago, New York, and Rome, the Scalabrini Sisters were like surrogate mothers to us. They handled all the domestic duties such as providing us with three wholesome meals a day, washing and mending our clothes, etc. The Sisters looked upon their ministry to potential priests as a calling from God and they performed it with great love. Many years later I was

Fr. Primo and his altar boys, three of whom became priests: Frank Cerniglia (Archdiocese of Chicago); Fr. Angelo Calandra, C.S.

honored to conduct the funeral service in Chicago for Mother Gaetana who was superior of the four sisters who were the first to serve in our minor seminary when I was there. Later on as priest and bishop, I always enjoyed celebrating significant events in the life of the community as well as anniversaries of the Sisters in their Provincial house in Melrose Park.

I remember with great respect the three Scalabrinian priests who staffed our parish of Santa Maria Addolorata at the time of my youth. The pastor was Fr. Joseph Bernardi. He was the one who baptized me and gave me first Holy Communion. He was a kindly person who guided the parish ship through the turbulent waters of the Depression and World War II. One characteristic of his was that he smoked awful-smelling Italian Parodi cigars. They were given some rather uncomplimentary names at the time. Fr. Bernardi died at age fifty-six, two years after my priestly ordination. The second priest was Fr. Joseph Rizzi. He was the elder statesman of the group. On Saturdays when most of us kids went to confession, Fr. Rizzi was generally in one of the confessionals. His line was always the longest. He was a good confessor and gave sound spiritual guidance. The fact that he was also hearing-impaired may have helped increase the lines. Fr. Rizzi died one month after my ordination as priest. He was eighty-one years old.

Procession to the church for Christmas Midnight Mass, 1940.

The third priest was Fr. Primo Beltrame. He was the new kid on the block. He was in his late twenties and had charge of the altar servers who at that time were only boys. Fr. Primo took a real interest in his altar boys. One day, I spoke to Fr. Primo about wanting to be an altar boy. This was right after I made my First Communion. He told me that there were two requirements: First, I had to be tall and strong enough to transport the huge missal and its stand from the Epistle side to the Gospel side of the altar. This was the procedure in the universally standard Tridentine Mass. Secondly, I must learn all the responses in Latin which was the language in use at every Mass throughout the world. With a little bit of effort I was able to meet the first requirement. To help me with the second, Fr. Primo gave me a little red book with the Latin responses. Mom agreed to help me; the fact that she knew Italian made it quite easy for her. In fact, I was so impressed that at one point I asked her in Italian: "Ma, are you a priest?" For us children, mom was always referred to as "Ma" and dad was always "Pa". So having had "Ma" as my tutor, I was officially installed as an altar boy of Santa Maria Addolorata Church.

Besides the regular Masses, I liked serving funerals even while I was a student in Washington School—just a few blocks away from

Washington School, Grade 2: Who is the only one wearing suspenders?

home. The priest who performed the funeral would sign a card with the server's name on it asking that he be excused from school for those two hours. We would then bring the card to the principal and he would send us back to the classroom. A nice arrangement, I thought.

Fr. Primo would schedule all of our serving assignments and would keep a written record of whether we showed up or not. He rewarded perfect attendance by taking us out on picnics to such places as Garfield Park, the Lincoln Park Zoo, and Riverview Amusement Park (now defunct). At that time, Navy Pier was not as developed and popular as it is today.

One summer I missed an assignment and was excluded from an altar servers' picnic. Why? Because one day I had a choice of either serving at the evening devotion as per assignment or go across the street to Allied Park to watch a much-heralded baseball game. It was Chicago type baseball with the 16 inch ball and no gloves. Being a huge baseball fan, I decided to go see the game. ("The devil made me do it.") Of course, my parents thought I was in church the whole time. Luckily they never found out.

I enjoyed serving Mass on Sundays and evening services, such as the Friday evening novena in honor of the Sorrowful Mother during World War II, and the Tuesday evening devotion in honor of St. Anthony. All of us servers vied to serve weddings on Saturdays because the best man would always slip us a tip.

In 1939, Addolorata parish opened a parochial school beginning with grades 1–5. My sister Olga and I both qualified. I entered in grade four and Olga in grade three. My class was to be second graduating class in the history of the school except that I left the school after seventh grade. (A grammar school dropout?) Our teachers were all religious sisters of a community known as the Daughters of St. Mary of Providence (DSMP).

This community of Sisters was founded in Italy in 1882 by Don Luigi Guanella (now Blessed Guanella). Don Luigi had assisted St. John Bosco in his ministry to homeless children. This led him to found a community of sisters to care for young children with Down syndrome and other developmental disabilities. It was in 1913 that the Sisters opened their first foundation in Chicago. Today they administer several facilities in the Archdiocese of Chicago. How did these Sisters with such expertise in special education come to teach in our parochial school? Your guess is as good as mine.

When Mom took me and Olga to register in the school, I got to meet the Sisters. As compared to the young teachers I had in Washington School, to a nine-year-old, all these Sisters looked old. They probably were in their early thirties. How aging changes one's perspective! Today anyone under sixty-five looks young to me.

To this day I remember with great gratitude the Sisters who taught me in those four years: Sister Salvatore, in fourth and seventh grade, Sister Mary Stella in grade five, and her sibling Sister Rosina in grade six. My class consisted of thirty-six children. It is amazing how the Sisters managed that large class without a teacher's aide or modern scholastic resources. I remember some interesting incidents during my four years in parochial school.

During my first year, in grade four, I continued to enjoy serving daily morning Mass at 8:00 a.m. before school. There was no eating or drinking before Mass in those days. This joy of serving Mass soon turned into a desire to say Mass. For some time I had been collecting holy cards of saints which I put into an album. (I kept all my baseball cards in a separate album.) I confided this desire of mine to be a priest to my teacher Sister Salvatore. She was very excited about the possibility that some day one of her pupils might become a priest. She certainly prayed for me and encouraged me. However she was concerned that my fragile-looking body might not be able to withstand the rigors of seminary life. So she arranged to have the Sisters' cook, Sister Teresa, prepare me a snack of milk and cookies in the Sisters' school dining room during recess. Were any of the other students jealous? I tried not to let them know. Sister Salvatore was also very much concerned about my spiritual preparation. She gave me several religious books to read such as the lives of the saints and even *The Imitation of Christ*, a classic of spiritual theology but a bit over my head.

In the fall of 1939, the Archbishop of Chicago, Cardinal George Mundelein, passed away. Every Catholic school was asked to send a representative to the funeral in Holy Name Cathedral. Probably at the suggestion of Sister Salvatore, I was chosen to represent Santa Maria Addolorata School. I entered the Cathedral for the first time. I was awe-struck to see the body of the Cardinal in an elevated coffin wearing his episcopal attire. The priesthood attracted me even more and I even wondered what it might be like to be a bishop. Little did I know.

When I had Sister Salvatore again as my teacher in grade seven, my spiritual preparation continued. She asked me to write a sermon like the priest did in church on Sunday. I worked at this unusual bit of homework. Hopefully, my sermons later as a priest improved considerably.

By this time, I felt that serving Mass was not good enough. It was about time that I learned how to say Mass. After having dropped a few timely hints to my parents before Christmas, I was hoping to receive a daily Missal in Latin and English. Before Christmas my mother would carefully hide all the gifts in the pantry. Would my Missal be among them? Curiosity got the best of me. When mom was not around I went and opened one of the boxes. There it was. I quickly put it away. Now I was faced with the task of having to show excitement and emotion when all of us children opened our gifts after the Christmas Midnight Mass.

So now with Missal in hand it was time to get down to business and start practicing how to say Mass. Where would I set up the altar? Ours was a three-bedroom flat: one for mom and dad; one for my two sisters and one for my two brothers. I was the odd man out so I slept on the couch in the living room. I set up the altar in my sisters' room. My sister Olga helped me and I asked her to serve my Mass long before girls were permitted to serve Mass. (Was I a prophet?)

Olga agreed to serve. But I acted like Mr. Hot Shot with my ability to read the Latin. Olga could not so I scolded her. She broke out into tears. Many times I remembered that day with deep regret. Olga was such a good kid, and she idolized her older brother.

While I was still in parochial school, my parents wanted their children to improve their knowledge of Italian and also learn some Italian literature. When I was ten or eleven years old I attended an Italian language school. One year the teacher decided to put on a play. It was based on Carlo Collodi's classic, *Pinocchio*. For some reason I was assigned to play the role of Pinocchio, probably because I had the longest nose in the class. We worked on the production for many months. Finally it was performed at an auditorium on Ashland Avenue. Was it a success? I cannot remember either the size or the reaction of the audience. All I know is that I was never given any offers for an acting career. Incidentally, the boy who played the part of Mangiafuoco also later became a priest. I guess acting was not our thing. We two were not the only ones from the neighborhood who chose the priesthood. In my little parish, I personally know of six who were ordained priests and two young women who became DSMP Sisters.

One of the sadder moments in my young life took place in December of 1941. On Sunday, December 7, Pearl Harbor was attacked by the Empire of Japan. The death toll from that invasion was over 2,000, while over 1,000 were injured. The following day, I remember listening on the radio to the address of President Franklin Roosevelt referring to the attack as a "date which will live in infamy", and declaring war on Japan. From that day on, I hoped someday I would be able to visit the site of that national tragedy and pay a prayerful tribute to those who lost their lives to protect us. One day it happened. Shortly after I was named pastor of St. Stephen in Vancouver in 1971, my mom came to visit me and she took me on vacation to Hawaii where we visited this tragic landmark. We cannot forget these military people who sacrificed their lives to protect our country nor the veterans of all our wars who risked their lives for the same purpose.

While I was still in the parochial school, one of my best friends was Joe Mio, who together with my two "bodyguards", Ernie Favaro and Del Baggetto, rescued me from a conflict or two. We were classmates for all four years in the parochial school. Joe Mio lived a block or two from our house and he would come over often. Both my parents liked Joe very much. We did many things together. Very often Joe's mom used to bake bread. The aroma of her freshly baked bread alone caught many people's attention—especially mine. When Joe would tell me that his mom was baking bread, I asked him if I could walk him home from school. When we got into the house his mother would ask me, "Renzo, won't you like a piece of bread? I just took it out of the oven." What a question! She knew I would never turn down such an offer. My mom was a good cook but somehow there was something special about Mrs. Mio's bread.

Growing up in a tenement district had its upside. There was never any shortage of players for our games: football, baseball, tag, kick the can or whatever. Aberdeen Street was our favorite playing field. Not too many cars drove by in those days. We made up our own rules for the games. We had no uniforms or equipment. We had no regular teams or leagues. Teams were made up from the guys who showed up. No umpires or screaming mothers except those who came out to break up the game in time for supper. We played when we felt like it. No schedules of any kind. And we had plenty of fun.

Walking distance from our neighborhood was a chocolate factory named Bloomer's. During World War II, on some days before closing, the owners would take the chocolates that were unsuitable for packaging and put two or three of them in small manila envelopes. The workers would distribute them to neighborhood kids. Joe and I would often be in line. What a treat. We would see chocolates only at Christmas or a birthday. Today whenever I drive by the factory with its characteristic smell of chocolate, I say a prayer of thanks for all the Bloomer's people who were so kind to all of us poor kids about seventy years ago.

Neither Joe Mio nor I owned a bicycle. First of all, I had one bad experience on a bicycle and that was enough for me. It happened when I was in grade five. My mother had bought me a nice blue slack suit for my confirmation. My sponsor, Louie DiSilvestro, owned a bike and wanted to take me for a ride dressed as I was in my new blue slacks. I was seated on the horizontal bar. Everything was going along fine until he made a sharp turn on a gravel road. We skidded and I fell on the gravel. My knees were scraped and my new slacks ruined. That was it. No more bicycle rides for me.

Ruining those new blue slacks was more painful to me than the scraped knees. My mother had taken me to purchase this confirmation present on Maxwell Street—the mecca of all immigrant bargain hunters. With that purchase I was given a free Mickey Mouse watch—my first ever wristwatch. It even worked…for a while.

Joe Mio and I made our own means of transportation. It was a pushcart. It wasn't hard to make. Just a two-by-four, an orange crate, half of an old roller skate in the front and the other in the back, two pieces of wood for handle bars and voilà! We had our wheels. We would decorate the cart with a rabbit foot on the handle bars and some bottle caps in the front. Today's roller blades or skateboards are no match for our pushcart. For starters, it was really "cool" and very cheap to make.

In our neighborhood in those days there were two movie theaters, the Schindler and the Cameo. The Schindler was everyone's choice. Many kids would show up on Saturday afternoon. Most of them were Italians from the neighborhood. For some reason, some outsiders referred to the Schindler as the "garlic opera." We didn't care. We were quite open-minded. The movies were often cowboy pictures without violence as we know it today. The good guys wore the white hats while the bad guys wore black hats and scruffy beards. The outcome of the conflict was always the same. The guys in the white hats (and sometimes on white horses) always won.

Joe and I liked to go to the movies but we couldn't always afford to. So from time to time we were hired by the manager of the Schindler to distribute glossy flyers to the homes in the neighborhood. These were advertisements about the featured movies of the week. We called them "pluggers." Our pay was five or six free passes to the movies. Not a bad arrangement.

Joe and I and many others from the neighborhood would spend a few weeks every summer at the Chicago Commons Farm Camp in New Buffalo, Michigan. It was a big treat for us city kids to get away from the city on those hot summer nights. There we enjoyed swimming in the creek, hiking, hay rides, roasting marshmallows and telling spooky stories in the evening around the campfire, going to Sunday Mass in Three Oaks and after Mass going to the nearby candy store with a nickel to spend before boarding the bus to return to camp. Sometimes Fr. Primo came to the camp to say Mass for the Catholics (which comprised most of the campers).

Mr. Hildebrand owned a dairy farm adjacent to the camp. I used to love to watch him milk the cow. It was fascinating. One time I got too close and he facetiously squirted me with warm milk. Every morning two of the bigger boys would bring a ten-gallon container of fresh milk to the dining hall before the Pledge of Allegiance to the Flag and breakfast. It was an honor to be chosen to raise the Flag in the morning with the world in the throes of war.

There were always the baseball games against a nearby camp named Tell High. I was too young to play on the team but I did get to sing with the cheering squad. Our favorite cheer went something like this: "Rub-a-dub-dub, rub-a-dub-dub, we got Tell High in the tub;

wash 'em out, wring 'em out, hang 'em on a line, we can beat Tell High any ole time." Real good sports, eh?

Life at camp was loads of fun. It sure beat turning on the fire hydrants in the city street to cool off the neighborhood. Obviously the firemen did not like that.

Even after I left home for the seminary, Joe and I would keep in touch. When I would come home for vacation in the summer, we would get together at a soda fountain and Joe would fill me in on all the doings of the kids in our class from Addolorata School.

With best friend Joe Mio (L) and "bodyguard" Ernie Favaro (R).

After high school, Joe enlisted in the Marines. I was so proud of him and happy that he came out of the service alive and well. He later married Betty and they had four children. When on vacation, I would visit him and his family in their home near Wrigleyville. As an inveterate Sox fan, that is about as close as I cared to be to Wrigley Field. However, there was something I enjoyed about Wrigley—the Wrigley Spearmint Chewing Gum. A pack cost only a nickel in those days. Joe was very proud when I returned to Chicago to celebrate Mass as bishop. Joe passed away in 1997.

After I left Santa Maria Addolorata School to enter the seminary, I continued to be in contact with the three DSMP sisters who taught me in elementary school. I would make it a point to visit them on my vacations from the seminary. They were elated when I was ordained a priest in 1957. Sister Salvatore sent me in Rome a hand-painted ribbon which was used to bind my hands after the anointing. The Sisters were equally elated when I was consecrated bishop in 1978. When Sister Salvatore retired from teaching she had an office in St. Mary of Providence School on Austin Avenue. On her desk she kept a picture of me in my bishop's robes. The Superior told me that whenever anyone went in to see her, she would point to the picture and say: "That's my little boy, Lorenzo." (little all right—all 200 pounds of him.) In 1988 Sister Salvatore passed away. I felt so indebted to her that I went to Chicago from Kamloops to preside at her funeral. She is buried in the Sisters' cemetery in Lake Zurich.

Sister Rosina, my sixth grade teacher, was a gentle soul with a beautiful smile and easy manner. On one of my visits to Chicago, I was able to see her when she was in Chicago on assignment. After she retired, she went to live in the Sisters Retirement Home in Lake Zurich. I went to visit her there. She invited me to join her for the 60th anniversary of her religious profession. Unfortunately, I was not able to attend. Instead I sent her a large bouquet of roses. She liked them so much she had a picture taken of her holding the roses and smiling. Her superior told me that she placed the roses in the chapel and tended them so diligently that they lasted much longer than usual. She died in 1991.

Sister Rosina (DSMP), my Grade 6 teacher, with the roses for her anniversary.

Sister Rosina's sister, Sister Mary Stella, my fifth grade teacher, was quite another story. She was different from Sister Rosina. In fact, I cannot think of any unusual thing that happened in sixth grade. We were pretty well behaved. Of course, the reason is that Sister Mary Stella in grade five had domesticated us.

Sister Mary Stella was more of a law and order type. Naturally, she had to deal with a large class of 36 rambunctious youngsters. I can attest to that as you will see from the following episode. Among other things, Sister Mary Stella was the time-keeper of the school. At that time there were no electronic bells in the school. Our activities were governed by the ringing of a huge cow bell. Sister would ring it in the stairwell at the appropriate times. It would resound through all three floors of the school. For easy access, Sister kept the bell right atop her desk. For some time I had been looking at the bell with some degree of curiosity. I wondered what would happen if I rang the bell at some inappropriate time. I would soon find out. When Sister was out of the room, I went to the desk, took the bell and proceeded to the stairwell. I rang the bell just the way Sister did and quickly replaced it on Sister's desk. Panic set in. All the teachers scrambled around and thought it might be a fire alarm. Suddenly Sister came huffing and puffing into the class and yelled out: "Who did that?" Honest Abe that I was, I raised my hand. First mistake. She grabbed me by the neck, dragged me to the blackboard and pushed my head against it several times. She then had me extend my hands and proceeded to bang me on the palms of my hand with a three pointed ruler. After this ordeal I returned to my desk humbled and with hands aching. I apologized for my bad behavior. Today some people would call this type of discipline an act of child abuse worthy of prosecution. Later I came to understand that it was rather a matter of "spare the rod and spoil the child" or simply a case of "tough love."

I went home from school that day looking for some sympathy from my mother. Second mistake. When I told her what had happened, she read me the riot act but never used corporal punishment. Her loud voice and demeanor were enough for me. I escaped the famous "barabim-barabom". I think I learned my lesson for the time being.

After I left the school in 1943, I was never able to see Sister Mary Stella in my visits to Chicago because she was always assigned to different parts of the country. However, in 1978, shortly after my consecration as bishop, I returned to celebrate a Pontifical Mass in my home parish of Santa Maria Addolorata. I went to see the Sisters at St. Mary's and was told that Sister Mary Stella was confined to bed upstairs in the nursing facility. She was in and out of consciousness and unable to speak. I was told that if I went to see her she would probably not recognize me, especially after 35 years. I decided to go anyway. I saw her there lying in bed, immobile and with her eyes closed. I went up to her and said: "Sister Mary Stella, do you remember me? I'm Lorenzo. I was one of your pupils in grade five. I came to thank you for putting up with me for that year and to apologize for my bad behavior." Quite unexpectedly, she opened her eyes slowly and I expected to see a look of panic in her eyes when she heard the name "Lorenzo". Instead she had a very peaceful look in her eyes. I took her hand and told her that I had just been consecrated a bishop and I came to give her my episcopal blessing. She gently squeezed my hand. As I blessed her, tears slowly ran down her cheeks. At that moment I knew that she recognized me and was indeed happy to see that her troublesome pupil was now a bishop. She died a year later.

When I was the Auxiliary Bishop of Vancouver, I had the opportunity to visit many of the local parishes. I learned that there were a number of Down Syndrome children and other children with special needs. I told the Archbishop about the DSMP's who were trained in special education. I asked him if he was interested in inviting this religious community to the Archdiocese. He agreed. In 1981 the Sisters opened their first foundation in British Columbia. They began a program called VANSPEC, namely, Vancouver Special Education.

They have since opened several satellite offices in the outlying areas of the Archdiocese.

After I was installed as bishop of Kamloops in 1982, I requested the DSMP's to come to the diocese. They agreed and for years did very fine pastoral work as special education religious teachers and pastoral associates.

After my retirement as bishop, I returned to Chicago and was very happy to be present at a special Mass in St. Mary's in 2005 on the occasion of the 90th anniversary of the Sisters' arrival in Chicago.

Another community of sisters who were very active in ministry to emigrants were the Missionary Sisters of the Sacred Heart (MSC) commonly known as the Cabrini Sisters. Their founder is St. Frances Cabrini, who was born in Italy in 1850. Mother Cabrini founded her missionary congregation with the desire to send her Sisters to China. Bishop Scalabrini, who was her contemporary, felt that her Italian community would be more useful in the United States among the hundreds of thousands of Italians who had emigrated there. Bishop Scalabrini was able to persuade Pope Leo XIII that she would be more needed in the United States at that critical time in history. So when Mother Cabrini went to see Pope Leo XIII to tell him of her plans, he told her, "Not to the East, but to the West." As a loyal daughter of the Church, she complied. She had already been apprised by Bishop Scalabrini of the difficult conditions of Italian immigrants in the United States. In 1889 Mother Cabrini left for New York with six of her Sisters. When they arrived, it was the Scalabrinian Fathers who provided a place for them in the now defunct St. Joachim's Church. From there they began their work among the poor immigrants. Their ministry quickly began to spread throughout the United States and other countries in Europe and Central and South America. In 1909 Mother Cabrini became an American citizen and died in Chicago's Columbus Hospital in 1917. Mother Cabrini was declared Blessed in 1938 and in 1946 she became the first United States citizen to be canonized a saint.

When I was a young boy, people were still talking about this Mother Cabrini. She was considered a saint by those who knew her personally.

A year after her beatification, Fr. Primo from our parish asked me if I would like to serve his Mass in the room of Columbus Hospital where Mother Cabrini died. I was excited to do so. The hospital no longer exists but the room where she died is still retained as a Shrine to this much-loved saint. In 1946 when she was declared a saint by Pope Pius XII, the Archdiocese of Chicago had a special celebration in her honor in Soldier Field. I was a minor seminarian at that time, and I was so proud to walk in the procession on the field at that historic event.

When I was in the minor seminary, Bishop Charles Greco of Alexandria, Louisiana, came to visit us. He told us of his personal encounter with Mother Cabrini. At the time, he was a boy attending a parochial school in New Orleans. Mother Cabrini visited the school and singled out young Charles. She said to him: "Young man, one day you will be a priest and a bishop." And so it was. Her prophecy came through. He was ordained a priest and later consecrated bishop in the same year that Mother Cabrini was canonized. I always remembered that memorable visit.

In 1950, Pope Pius XII formally proclaimed St. Frances Xavier Cabrini the "Patroness of Immigrants."

Live in
harmony with
one another.

(Rom 12:16)

Meet the Sabatinis: My Father "Domingo" or Dominic

MY father was born in Brazil in 1901. His parents had emigrated there from Italy in the mid nineteenth century in the hope of a better life. My father was one of ten children. Most of his older siblings married and stayed in Brazil. When my grandparents retired, they returned to their little town of Valbona in the Garfagnana region of the province of Lucca.

Valbona is a very old small town situated about four hundred feet above sea level in the Appenine Mountains. It is built along the banks of the River Esarulo where my mother used to fish for trout when she was young. She told us that they were plentiful in her day. In 1951 when I went there for the first time, there was no road. Access was by foot or mule or horse from the nearest town of Castiglione about five miles away. The town dates back to the late Middle Ages. The original name of the town was "Il Piola" after my mom's ancestors. I often wondered why anyone would want to build a town so far from civilization. Were my ancestors smugglers who were trying to escape the law? This thought deterred me from any interest in a genealogical search for my family tree.

My father was a teenager at the time, so when his parents returned, they brought him back to Italy with them. It was there that he met and married Ada Pioli from Valbona in 1920. In 1924 they emigrated to Chicago with their two children. My Uncle Silvio Pioli and his wife Pasquina had emigrated to Chicago one year earlier. They had rented a three-story flat and occupied the third floor. Knowing from experience about the poor economic condition in Italy in general and the Garfagnana in particular, my uncle invited his sister Ada and family to join them. My family was to live on the second floor of the building. The first floor was an unoccupied storefront, at least for a time.

When this family of four came to Chicago, my father was offered a job as janitor at the Chicago Commons building on Grand Avenue and Morgan Street. When I was still a toddler, my father took me by the hand and walked me to the Chicago Commons. He wanted to show me his "office". His "office" was the furnace room in the basement of the building. In those days the heating fuel was coal. Delivery trucks would dump the coal on the sidewalk of the building. From there my father would shovel the coal through a small window into the coal bin. From the bin he would then shovel the coal into the huge furnace. Some "office" he had! When I had my first office as a priest, I often thought about my father's "office". He raised his family by working in his "office".

The people of the Chicago Commons were extremely good to the poor Italian immigrants and their children. They provided them with gifts and clothes as well as the use of their summer camp in New Buffalo, Michigan. In the summer of 1964, I visited the camp with Mom and brother Ralph and visited it again in August of 1987. My, how things changed since we went camping there in the late 30's! Among other things, the campers now had styrofoam mattresses instead of mattresses that we filled with straw when we arrived and emptied when we left. Every year we worked on a totem pole which, when completed, would be placed around the campfire site. Some of those totems were still standing in 1987—slowly rotting away. Now instead of swimming in a little creek, the campers had a beautiful outdoor swimming pool. Unfortunately, the camp was eventually closed.

In the backyard of our house, my father and Uncle Silvio had built a bocce court—the Italian equivalent of lawn bowling. During the summer months Pa and Silvio would play bocce with some of their friends. I enjoyed watching them as a boy and picked up a few Italian swear words along the way. They sure took their "bocce" games seriously. One day I walked into the house from the yard and to show how big I was, I repeated some of the words I had just heard on the "bocce" court. My mother gave me an earful and I never repeated those words again. I never liked the prospect of having my mouth washed out with soap, a common threat in those days.

In back yard with "bocce" court: L-R Joe, Mom, Ralph, Aunt Pasquina, and Olga. Lizzy's house in the background.

One day my father came home from work with a large box

filled with ice skates of various sizes. He gave the skates to us children and the neighborhood kids as well. In the cold winter nights, my father would flood the bocce court so we could all ice skate with our friends after supper under the lights. Having fun was not very complicated in those days.

Just beyond the bocce court there was an old dilapidated house where an elderly couple lived. I think they both drank a bit. At times I would see the husband going home from the local tavern with a pail of beer in his hand. It was not a peaceful household. At various times we would hear loud screams emanating from the house. The woman's name was Lizzy. She was a rather scary person. Sometimes when we played in the yard, we would see her, dressed in her black dress, peering at us from a window. She made me very uneasy. In fact, she caused me several nightmares.

Since our food budget was very restricted because of the Depression and the subsequent Second World War, my father raised rabbits in the basement of the house. On some Saturdays, when I was still a toddler, Pa would place me in his little red wagon and take me to the feed store where he would buy a bale of alfalfa for the rabbits. On the way home he would seat me on the alfalfa and I was so proud to view the surroundings from such a high perch.

On another occasion, Pa announced to me that the mother rabbit was going to have babies. I was very excited about that. After it happened, my father took me down to the basement and there they were—the mother and six baby rabbits. After a few moments, I asked my father that inevitable question: "Pa, where did the baby rabbits come from?" Without any hesitation my father said to me: "Renzo, do you see the big ears the mother has? The babies come out of the ears." The answer appeared quite reasonable to me…at least for a few years.

My father also made wine in the basement for private use only. In the fall, he would order several cases of choice grapes from California. He had a wine press and several oak barrels to store the wine for fermentation. I would go down to the basement to watch him and was fascinated to see the dark juice oozing through the openings in the press. One day my father lifted me up, put my hand on the steel bar and the two of us would move around the press. I was so proud. After all, I was helping my father make wine.

Several years later my father took me to visit the stockyards on the South Side. When the wind was blowing from the south, we could smell the pungent odor in our neighborhood. The stockyards opened in Chicago in 1865 and by the year 1900 it employed over one thousand people—mostly immigrants especially from Ireland and Germany. By 1940, years after my father brought me there, a total of close to one million animals moved through the stockyards. Several meat-packing companies established operations there, such as Armour, Swift and others. Chicago had gained a wide reputation as the beef capital of the United States. Eventually for many reasons the stockyards were closed in 1971.

My visit there while I was a youngster is one I would rather not remember. The stench and the piercing cries of those frightened animals being slaughtered while standing on blood-soaked floors was just too much for me. That scene lingered within me for years and aroused in me a terrible distaste for the killing of innocent animals, especially for sport.

My father was a very good, hard-working parent who loved his children. After work, as tired as he was, he always found time to play with us before supper. Supper in the Sabatini household was a sacred ritual. It took place precisely at 6:00 p.m. I know because I would have to turn off the radio after listening to those serials such as *Jack Armstrong, the All-American Boy* or *Captain Midnight*. The staple food for us Tuscans was polenta. It was a version of corn meal. In those days, there were no instant foods so Ma had to stir the polenta in this huge kettle for quite a while. It was tiring so as soon as my father would return from work and enter the house, I would hear my mom say to him: "Domingo, mesta la polenta."—"Dominic, stir the polenta" and my father would oblige, as tired as he was. Polenta, which was the staple of poor people, is now a gourmet dish served in some Italian restaurants.

The kids in the neighborhood liked my father. In the summer after supper, Pa would sit on a chair in front of the house and the kids, including my pal Joe Mio, would stop to hear some of Domingo's stories in broken English.

Birthdays were always special in our house. It was time for a party with family and friends with a birthday cake and a gift that we dearly longed for. On one of my birthdays, my parents gave me a miniature football. They knew I was a great football fan and liked playing football. It was a great gift. The football was small and very light. I could grip my little hands around it and throw spirals. One day I was playing with the football on Aberdeen Street with some of my

My ninth birthday party: L-R Aunt Pasquina, Mae, Uncle Silvio; L standing) Mr. Jenns, Joe's sponsor for Confirmation; next to Joe, Irene D'Agostino and brother Syl; seated Dad, Olga, Mom and Jenny.

friends from the neighborhood. The ball landed in the middle of the street. Along came a milk truck. It was not the horse-and-buggy type. By this time the delivery trucks were motorized. The passing truck drove right over the football and completely crushed it. That was the end of the football season for us. Birthdays come only once a year.

One time I said to my father: "Pa, you're from Brazil, aren't you? Isn't that where nuts come from?" Fortunately, my father did not get the gist of it.

My father was a homebody. He rarely went out except to visit friends and then it was with the whole family. Before my oldest brother Ralph left for the Army, one day the three of us boys asked Pa if the four of us could go out together. After all, Mom and the two girls went out together for shopping sometimes, so why couldn't the four of us go out for a good time? We decided to take Pa to the movies. He had hardly ever been in a theatre but he consented. We took the Milwaukee Avenue streetcar to the Congress Theater and saw a double feature: "The Flying Tigers" and "The Road to Morocco." How happy we were to see Pa laugh every time he recalled some of the comical scenes in that Bing Crosby and Bob Hope movie. That day out remained fixed in my memory till this day. It would be the last time that the four of us would ever go out together. My brother Ralph would soon be going off to war and I would be entering the seminary.

In 1948, a few years after World War II ended, my father had saved up enough money to take a trip by himself to Italy to visit his father whom he had not seen since coming to the States 24 years before. Grandpa was in his eighties at the time and my father was 45 years old.

What was supposed to be a happy reunion did not turn out that way. After just one week, on October 1, 1948, my father died from a blood clot in the leg. Doctors and medical technology were not easily available in those days especially in small remote towns. His funeral took place in the parish church where he had married. His body lies at rest in the local cemetery next to members of his family.

Obviously I was completely devastated when I was given the news. The last time I saw my father was in that summer of 1948 just before he left for Italy. I was preparing to leave Chicago for the Scalabrinian novitiate on Staten Island. My father had told me that on his return to the States after visiting with his father and siblings, he would stop to visit with me in New York for a few days. Being away from home and family for the first time, I was anxiously awaiting my father's visit. He would then be able to see me wearing my novice's cassock. But the reunion never happened. I was permitted to go home to Chicago for Pa's memorial Mass in Santa Maria Addolorata Church and a brief visit with the family. My heart was in turmoil. I was struggling with the idea of either going back to the novitiate or abandoning the idea of continuing my studies for the priesthood and stay home to help mom and siblings. My mother must have sensed my dilemma so at table after the Mass she said to me: "Renzo, if you really feel that God is calling you to be a priest, go back to the novitiate. Don't worry about us. God will look after us." And indeed He did. Later on, trusting in her culinary skills, Ma opened a family restaurant in Lake County that proved quite successful.

My Mother Ada

My mother was born in the town of Valbona in Italy on January 26, 1899. Like my father's parents, Ma's parents had also emigrated to Brazil. There they had four sons who eventually married and remained in Brazil. When Grandma was pregnant with my mother she went to Italy. She wanted her child to be born there rather than in those primitive conditions in the backwoods of Brazil where my grandfather worked. When Grandma rejoined her family in Brazil, my mother was raised by a relative in Valbona. As a young girl my mother was very close to her parish church. She looked after it with great devotion. The local parish priest was a frequent visitor in the Pioli home. He loved playing cards with the family and friends. Ma was a woman of great faith. After arriving in Chicago, she continued to practice her faith. She and my father walked with us to church every Sunday. Ma would teach us our prayers and made sure we would recite them every night before falling asleep. I would sometimes hear mom and dad reciting their prayers together in their room.

Mom had a great love and respect for priests. Our parish priests and other Scalabrinians were always welcome guests in the Sabatini household for dinner or simply for a friendly visit.

Ma was a stay-at-home mom and looked after us with tender love and devotion. We never knew the meaning of the word baby-sitter. One day when I was still a toddler, I remember what my mother said to me when we heard the church bells toll for a funeral. She was mending some clothes. She said to me: "Renzo, be quiet. Mass is going on in church." Then she would pause for a few minutes to pray.

At that age I had no clue what Mass was all about except that when those bells rang, something important must be going on in church.

Ma would do all the chores in the house: cooking, baking, making pasta, washing clothes with an old scrubbing board and an old washing machine. She mended our socks and clothes and made sure that no matter how poor we were, we were always clean and tidy.

When my sister Olga and I were still in Washington School, Mother would prepare our lunch which consisted of a peanut butter and jelly sandwich or a balogna sandwich or the like. She would give us two cents apiece for a carton of milk. We could not afford the luxury of chocolate milk. It cost three cents.

When we would come home from school, Mom was always there to greet us with a hug and kiss and a glass of milk and a few of her delicious homemade "biscotti." I cannot remember one day when Mom was not at home waiting for us after school. There were no latchkey kids in our neighborhood.

There was certainly no secret in our house when Ma was making pasta. Every conceivable flat surface in the house was lined with thick slices of pasta. When it was dry, Ma would cut it into thinner slices like spaghetti or linguini.

The period of the Second World War was a time of serious restraint for all Americans. Many items such as sugar, meat, butter, and gasoline were rationed. Many people had victory gardens, as they were called then. Mom and Dad had one of their own. Someone had offered them a plot of land further northwest and they would take the Milwaukee Avenue streetcar. They hoed the land, seeded it and watered it, and in the summer they would pick the vegetables and spices and come home with shopping bags full of produce like so many Italians did in those days. Sometimes they would take me with them—just for company! One day I asked my mom if I could have my own victory garden in the back yard. I promised her I would weed it and water it. She agreed so I had my own plot about three feet by six feet. I was so excited when I picked my first carrot and showed it to Ma. It felt great to be helping the war effort!

It was also during the war that my parents bought our first ever automobile. It was a Chevrolet that was bought from a man who was drafted into the service. He was anxious to sell it before leaving for war. We were so proud of our car. My father even built a garage in the yard to protect it. It was quite a treat when the family went out for a Sunday drive.

Although I was away from home for most of my life, I still had numerous occasions to spend quality time with Ma. She and my dear little sister Olga came to my first religious profession in Staten Island, New York on September 8, 1949.

In 1951 when I was assigned to continue my studies in Rome, some friends drove Ma and me by car to New York. We made a stopover to visit Niagara Falls. Having lived in New York already for three years, I was pleased to show them some of the famous attractions in the Big Apple before I was to leave for Rome by boat on the U.S.S. *Constitution*.

In 1953, Mom came to Italy for the first time since emigrating from there in 1924. I took her to visit my father's grave in Valbona, the town where she was born and grew up. She also met many of our relatives and friends. Mom dearly loved her poor hometown of Valbona, which is now almost deserted. When we were children, she used to say to us: *Dopo Roma viene Valbona*,—i.e., "After Rome comes Valbona." The Italians have a word for this. They call it *campanelismo*—pride in the place of the church bells. Mom also quoted to us another of her many Italian proverbs: *"Guai a quell'ucciello che in cattiva valle nasce."* "Woe to that bird who is born in a bad valley." It just keeps going back.

My mother came again to Rome in March of 1957 for my ordination to the priesthood, after which we went to her church of Valbona for my first Solemn High Mass. By the time I went back to

Rome for further studies, Mom was then pretty much on her own. Her four children married within the space of two years: Olga in 1952, Ralph and Jenny in 1953 and Joe in 1954.

In a subsequent visit to Rome in 1959 when I was doing graduate work, Ma was thrilled to visit the Pope's summer home in Castelgandolfo and have an audience with Pope John XXIII. Ma really loved "Papa Giovanni" and was saddened by his death in 1963.

After I completed my studies in Rome in 1960, I was assigned to the faculty of St. Charles Seminary in New York. I would return to Chicago for vacation and spent much time with Ma and the family. She took me with her on vacation to Italy, Brazil and other parts of the world. It was in August of 1962 that we made our first trip together to Brazil to visit Ma's two surviving brothers and other relatives.

Ma would come to visit me in British Columbia for my birthday almost every year. A few times she was not able to come because of illness. I would go to celebrate my birthday with her in Chicago and say Mass in her home. In 1979, I was in Chicago to celebrate Ma's eightieth birthday with family, relatives and friends in her parish of St. Bede's in Ingleside. This occasion would be the last time that all six members of the Sabatini family would be photographed together. I tried to get to Chicago to visit Ma and family whenever I could. I would travel from British Columbia to Ottawa several times a year for Bishops' meetings. On my return, I would take a detour to Chicago and spend a few days there with the family.

Mom's 80th birthday party. L-R Olga, Jenny, Joe and Ralph.

My Sister Jenny

Jenny was born in Valbona, Italy in 1922. She was the oldest child and helped Ma raise us little ones. The financial situation in the home was rather tight in the 30's. After Jenny graduated from Wells High School, she was looking for a job in order to help the family. The first floor of our building was an empty store front. My family decided to rent the space and opened a diner for breakfast and lunch. It was called the "Erie Sandwich Shop." Across the street from our house was a huge factory with numerous employees. Jenny managed the store and had some help from her neighborhood friends. The business was an instant success and greatly improved the fortunes of the family. Hence, Olga and I would come home for lunch and did not have to pack our peanut butter sandwiches to take to school.

Jenny always treated me well. She was eight years older than I and was like a second mother to me. She would take me shopping downtown by streetcar and then treat me to a fudgy-wudgy at Woolworth's Drug Store.

Jenny knew that I loved football and was an ardent fan of the Fighting Irish of Notre Dame. My idol was quarterback Angelo Bertelli who later went on to win the Heisman Trophy. One Christmas Day when dinner was over, Jenny took me downtown to the McVickers Theater to see the movie *Knute Rockne—All American*. I thoroughly enjoyed it. It was a great Christmas present.

Jenny also knew that I loved baseball. She was able to persuade one of the neighborhood "boys" with tickets to take me to my first ever major league baseball game. It was in Wrigley Field which was fairly new and very beautiful in those days. By that time I was already a Sox fan but who cares? It was my first professional game. I don't remember very much about the game except that the Cubs were playing the Pittsburgh Pirates and the centerfielder for the Pirates was Vince DiMaggio, the least known of the three DiMaggio brothers.

Shortly before I entered the seminary, Jenny took us kids downtown to see the stage production of Irving Berlin's *This is the Army* featuring Berlin himself. During the war in 1942 Berlin had started a revue with a cast of 350 servicemen who toured the country. I was thrilled to be able to see him when he came to Chicago. I had already seen the movie *Holiday Inn*, which featured Bing Crosby singing Berlin's popular song "White Christmas". Berlin also gave us "God Bless America". This stage production tweaked my interest in Broadway musicals. In fact, during my time in New York in the 60's, I was able to see several fine musical productions. It was also in the decade of the 60's that I developed an interest in Italian opera. I saw my first Italian opera "Rigoletto" by Giuseppe Verdi in the old New York Metropolitan Opera House. This was the same stage on which world-known opera stars performed such as Enrico Caruso, Maria Callas, Renata Tebaldi and many others. When the Opera House was moved to Lincoln Center, I felt that it lost some of the unique character of the Old Met with its marvelous acoustics.

Jenny was always there for me when I needed her. When we

founded a youth drug prevention center in a rented storefront on Staten Island in the late 60's, Jenny and her husband Bruno Michelotti organized a fund-raiser to help us with the rent. She and Bruno were married in 1953 while I was in Rome. They had three children, the late Roger, Lori and Linda. I was happy to celebrate Bruno and Jenny's 25th wedding anniversary on April 25, 1978. They later came to visit me in Kamloops several times. We even went on vacation together to visit our relatives in Brazil.

Jenny was very pleased when I retired and returned to Chicago in 1999. I visited her often in her home and later in Sunrise Assisted Living in Bloomingdale. I would often take her out for lunch to Portillo's which was across from Sunrise.

It was early in the year 2001 that Jenny's health began to deteriorate and I tried to visit her more often. In December her condition became critical and I went to see her to give her the anointing of the sick and to pray for her. I was there together with her family on December 20 when she passed away. She is buried with her husband and son Roger in Christ the King Mausoleum in Hillside.

My Brother Ralph

When I was a boy, my oldest brother Ralph and I were very close. He was always interested in what I was doing and what my plans were.

After Ralph graduated from Wells High School he enrolled in the University of Illinois in Champaign-Urbana. During that time, one Saturday Notre Dame was scheduled to play Illinois in Champaign. Ralph asked me if I would like to go down and see the game. What a rhetorical question! He knew full well that I listened to the Notre Dame games every Saturday on the radio but had never seen a live game. Ralph had a ticket for me and so there I was seated among all those college students in their orange and blue jerseys while I waved my green and gold Notre Dame banner. At half-time Illinois was leading Notre Dame. The Illinois students seated around us kept teasing me. But in the second half Notre Dame came back to win the game. I had the last laugh. As we exited the stadium, I proudly waved my Notre Dame banner as high as I could.

Ralph was drafted into the army and was stationed in Europe. At that time I was already in the minor seminary. Ralph would write to me regularly on those postal aerograms. Ralph told me how proud he was that I was following my dream of wanting to be a priest. Ralph returned from the war in December of 1945. The day after his return,

After Easter Mass in front of Erie Sandwich Shop. L-R: Olga, Jenny, Ralph, Ma and Joe

he came to visit me in the seminary. Together with the rest of the family, I had prayed every day for his safe return and I was so excited to see him again. While in the seminary I missed my family, especially during the holidays.

Ralph married Florence Ecklund in 1953 and they had two children, Ralph Jr. and Tom. When I returned to the States in 1960 during my vacation I would spend many hours in the evening with my brother chatting over some wine and cheese and fresh fruit. We got along so well, just like when I was a boy. In turn, Ralph and his wife Florence visited me in Vancouver and Kamloops several times. Ralph was so proud when I was ordained a priest and doubly proud when I was named a bishop. He could not do enough for me. He took me to a clerical clothier to purchase my purple robes and all the other necessary episcopal accoutrements.

Unfortunately, in January of 1984 my brother Ralph was diagnosed with lung cancer. Eventually the cancer spread throughout his body. He was in terrible pain but refused to take morphine. He wanted to be fully alert and be able to communicate with family and friends. I would phone him regularly and come to visit him from Kamloops as often as I could. He was always so happy to see me. We were that close.

But Ralph also had many close friends, among them Fred and Dolores Nagel. Ralph and the Nagels were among the first people from Chicago to visit me in Vancouver when I was assigned there in 1971. Fred and Dolores went to see my brother very regularly during his eleven-month battle with cancer. When I returned to Chicago and was pastor of Holy Rosary, Fred and Dolores and their daughter Karen became fond of the parish. They joined the annual banquet committee and helped us in many ways.

In December of 1984 Ralph's condition worsened. He was bedridden and had nurse's care in his home twenty-four hours a day. One evening I had the feeling that he was dying. I phoned the house and the nurse answered. I asked her how he was doing. She said that he was critical but that I could talk to him. I did but I could tell that his condition was very poor. I told the nurse that I was taking the very first flight out of Kamloops and asked her if she thought he would still be alive when I got there. She said to me: "Oh, don't worry about that. He said he is waiting for you." On December 14, I took the early morning flight to Chicago, rented a car and drove to my brother's house in Ingleside. It was about 2:00 p.m. My brother was so happy to see me and, as weak as he was, we talked just as we used to do. He had already received the Sacraments so I asked him if he would like to receive the Holy Viaticum. He said "yes" so I phoned the local parish and the priest brought the Eucharist which I gave to him. Together with family and friends we said the prayers for the dying and at 5:00 p.m. he passed away. The nurse who had been assisting him said to me with tears in her eyes: "I have been at the bedside of many dying people but I have never seen such a beautiful death as this one." I had lost my brother and my very close friend. I celebrated his funeral Mass and I thanked God that I could be at his bedside in that critical hour.

My Brother Joe

My brother Joe was born in Chicago in 1927. There is very little I remember of Joe from our childhood except that there was definitely a case of sibling rivalry between us and I probably was the real culprit. Here is an incident that comes to mind. Ma knew I loved cherries so before I came home from the minor seminary for summer vacation, she would buy a whole box of cherries. She gave strict orders to Joe and everyone else: "No one is to open that box until Renzo comes home." Joe resented this because he felt that she was showing favoritism to me which she obviously was. When Joe would speak to Ma about me, he would refer to me as "your little priest." He felt he was older than I and deserved more respect. In any case, when I did come home, he would be sure to tell me that he got into the cherries before I did. There, take that!

There is another incident that I remember. I don't know if Joe was terribly excited about my wanting to be a priest. One day I went with one of my cousins to the State-Lake Theater which at that time was across the street from the Chicago Theater. The State-Lake showed not only a movie but also a stage show. The day I went, the stage show featured an all-girl band. When I told Joe about it, he was quick to tell me: "So you went to see a stage show with a whole bunch of girls performing in short dresses? And you want to be a priest? Yeah, right."

But the rivalry did not last long because when the chips were down, Joe was always there for me. After Joe graduated from

Audience with Pope Pius XII with brother Joe and soldier friends.

Washington School, our parents insisted that he receive a Catholic High School education. He attended Fenwick High School in Oak Park. After graduation, he went to Washburne Trade School, where he took chef training. Later, when the family opened a restaurant named "Sabatini's" on the shore of Long Lake in Lake County, Ma and Joe were the chief chefs. Not long after, he was drafted in the Army and he and mom came to visit me in the seminary in New York. I was so proud to see him in uniform. In 1952 when I was studying in Rome, Joe was stationed in southern Germany. In February of that year he drove down to Rome by jeep with a group of other soldiers and he came to visit me. He was the first family member I saw since I had left for Rome in 1951. I took my brother and his soldier friends to the Vatican and we had an audience with Pope Pius XII. We were all thrilled when the Pope personally gave us a papal medal. I would meet up with Joe again the following summer when we visited our many relatives in Garfagnana as well as some of the major cities of Italy.

One year during my vacation I went to visit him in the Army camp near Garmisch in the Bavarian Alps. I had never been to an army camp, and I enjoyed seeing all those soldiers. I had lunch with them in the soldiers' mess and the food was good.

In 1954 Joe married Virginia Petitti and they had one daughter, Lisa.

When I was consecrated Auxiliary Bishop in 1978, Joe was proud of his little brother. When I went to Valbona to celebrate Mass in the same church where I said my first Solemn Mass as a priest twenty-one years before, my brother Joe and Virginia came for the celebration. We had a great time together visiting relatives.

While I was bishop of Kamloops, Joe and his wife came to visit me four times. The last time was in August of 1988. During that month, the movie actor and director Martin Sheen came to Kamloops with his two sons, Charlie Sheen and Emilio Estevez, to film a movie called *Cadence*. The name Estevez was the original family name. Martin changed the name to Sheen because of his admiration for Bishop Sheen, the well known preacher and TV personality.

After Sunday evening Mass in Cathedral with Martin Sheen and parishioners. Standing, second from right, Fr. Dale.

During the filming, Martin and some of the cast would come to the Cathedral every Sunday for the 7:00 p.m. Mass. One of the actors was brought to the faith by Martin and was baptized in Assisi. This actor was an excellent organist. He was invited to play at one of the Sunday evening Masses and made the Church rock. Martin invited me and my brother and his wife to come to the set to watch the filming. It was quite a new experience for us and a special thrill especially for Virginia. We got to meet Martin and his son Charlie and have lunch with the other actors and crew.

When the filming was completed, I invited Martin to meet with our youth in the Cathedral hall after his last Sunday Mass in Kamloops. He agreed. As I escorted him into the room, all those many anxious young people began to swoon. I turned to Martin and was about to say to him jokingly: "Don't be shocked, Martin, they do this to me every time I walk in the room." Yeah, fat chance!

Joe and Virginia and I spent several vacations together. When Joe's wife passed away in 1998, his life would never be the same. Joe's health began to weaken. He was in and out of the hospital several times.

When I retired and came back to Chicago in 1999, I would spend time with him in his home and we had some very intimate conversations. I got to know him much better than when we were growing up. In 2001 his health got so bad that he was admitted as a resident in Villa Scalabrini in Northlake where the Scalabrinian Sisters and staff ministered to him in a truly loving way. I would go to visit him almost every day. I would walk him through the halls in his wheelchair until one day he was confined to bed in a very serious state. He received all the Sacraments and we said the prayers of the dying. He passed away that same day. It was November 28, 2001. I was happy to be with him when the Lord called him back home. Another sibling gone. As a brother, priest and bishop it was a privilege for me to celebrate his funeral Mass.

My Sister Olga

My future little altar server was born in 1931. There was something unique about her birth. All of Ma's children were born at home with the help of the neighborhood midwife. Ma was on her way to the hospital by cab for Olga's birth and claimed that Olga was born before they reached the hospital. Olga was the baby of the family and she and I were very close not only in age but also in spirit. Olga did not like school very much. She had a difficult time with the Sisters in the parochial school. When she graduated, my parents insisted that she attend a Catholic high school notwithstanding her difficulties with the Sisters. Olga survived one year at Siena High School in River Forest and eventually got her wish to go to a public school. Olga married Charles Leiser and they had two children, Nadine and Charles Jr. By this time Olga had developed a good relationship with some of the Sisters in her parish in Schiller Park. Apparently a conversion took place. Olga and Charlie were married while I was a seminarian in Rome, but I was pleased to celebrate their 25th wedding anniversary on October 28, 1977.

Olga had a mortal fear of flying. She was never on a plane. When I was to be consecrated bishop, she said she would risk it and fly to Vancouver. She made it without incident and was so happy to be an active part of the celebration. Maybe she felt safe because on the same plane from Chicago there were about twenty priests, most of them Scalabrinians, in their clerical suits going to my consecration. It was said that when this group of priests exited the airport, one person in the crowd waiting for a passenger said out loud: "Gee, I didn't think that Vancouver needed salvation that badly." Quite a statement. I'm not going there.

When Olga's husband Charlie retired as Chief of the Fire Department of Schiller Park, the two of them decided to sell their home. They relocated in Branson, Missouri near the Ozark Lake. Charlie loved to fish. But unfortunately Olga would not live to enjoy her new home for very long.

In July of 1988, she was diagnosed with cancer. It spread very quickly through her body. I would phone her regularly from Kamloops and realized that her condition was poor, and I was not going to take any chances. One day I phoned and told her that I was going to fly down to see her and say Mass for her in her house. The very next morning I took the plane from Kamloops to Springfield, Missouri. I rented a car and drove to her home in Branson. She was so happy to see me. I said Mass in the home for her and her husband Charlie. They received Holy Communion and afterwards Olga was barely strong enough to prepare dinner for the three of us. We then visited for a while. The following morning Charlie and I put her in the car and drove her to the hospital for another treatment of chemotherapy. I sat at her bedside for several hours. I looked at her and noticed the change in her. She was no longer that beautiful girl with natural blond hair and blue-green eyes. She was running a high fever. Her husband and I decided to fly her to Chicago so she could be with her two children. The doctors would not allow her to be moved until she was without fever for at least 24 hours. I prayed very hard that the fever would subside. It did. She was put on a plane and flown back to Chicago to be with her children. Her condition continued to get worse.

One day I talked to her on the phone and something inside told me that she would not last much longer. Her husband said to me that she wasn't that critical and it was not necessary for me to make the trip so soon. I did not agree. I took the first flight out of Kamloops and arrived in Chicago in early afternoon. My sister Jenny and her husband Bruno were there to meet me at the airport. They told me that Olga died three hours ago while the plane was still in flight. I was so deeply saddened. We were so very close, yet I was not with her when she passed away. I said Mass in the house for the family and later conducted her funeral Mass in her local parish church. But the pain in my heart lingered. She would be my only sibling at whose bedside I failed to be in that last critical hour and she was so close to me in life. She was fifty-seven when she died. But I know that Olga is O.K. She led a good life.

Beloved, if God
so loved us, we
also ought to
love one another.

(1 Jn 4:11)

Meet the Piolis: Silvio

MA's brother Silvio, who was born in Brazil, and his wife Pasquina had three children: Giuseppe (Joe), Dino (Don) and Amabile (Mabel or Mae). Joe and Don were born in Italy while Mae was born in Chicago. The Pioli family and ours were very close not only because they lived upstairs from us but also because Ma and uncle Silvio had no other relatives in the United States. We were like an extended family, very often enjoying a Sunday meal together after church. We went on picnics together and shared the same friends. Uncle Silvio loved bowling and so did I. When I was home for vacation and staying at Long Lake, I would often drive to his home in McHenry and the two of us would go out bowling. Uncle Silvio was a very funny guy and laughed heartily at good jokes. In 1967, uncle Silvio came to see me on Staten Island for a few days after visiting his relatives in Brazil. One year later he passed away. I went to Chicago to celebrate the funeral Mass in his parish of St. Patrick's in McHenry. He is buried

Sunday dinner with Sabatini's and Piolis. Standing L-R: Dad, Ralph, Mae, Joe, Uncle Silvio and Aunt Pasquina. Seated L-R: Mom, Jenny, Olga, Joe Pioli, wife Ann, and two neighbors.

in the Queen of Heaven Mausoleum next to his wife Pasquina and now also my mother.

Pasquina Suffredini

Pasquina Suffredini-Pioli was a soft-spoken and very kind and gentle person. She was very good to all the Sabatini children. We missed her and the family when they moved from the third floor of our building to a home further west. Pasquina and Silvio had a summer cottage in Wonder Lake. The Sabatinis were often very welcome guests. We loved to go there because, like our Ma, Aunt Pasquina was a great cook. In the spring of 1963 Aunt Pasquina was diagnosed with cancer. When she took seriously ill, I flew to Chicago to visit her in Loretto Hospital. When she died I went to Chicago to do her funeral in Santa Maria Addolorata Church, which was her church, and, when she emigrated from Italy, also ours.

After the Piolis left Erie Street, their third floor flat was rented to Antonio and Agnese Palazzo, an Italian immigrant couple from Monopoli near Bari. Their only child, Isabella, was born while they lived upstairs from us. Little Isabella not only brought joy to her parents but also to all the Sabatinis who treated her as their own. Isabella went on to graduate from De Paul University in 1961. However, when her parents retired and decided to return to Italy in 1970, Isabella gave up her career and went back to Italy to look after her elderly parents. She did so far beyond the call of duty. She took to heart the words of the commandment: "Honor thy father and thy mother." On one of our trips to Italy, Mom and I went to Monopoli to visit the Palazzos in their beautiful high-rise apartment overlooking the Adriatic Sea. On that occasion, Isabella took us to visit the famous caves about twenty-five miles southeast of Bari. They are called the "Grotte di Castellana" and are quite a famous tourist attraction

Agnese passed away several years before her husband Antonio who lived to be 104. Isabella looked after both of them in their home all those many years. Talk about filial devotion.

When I celebrated my first Mass as a priest in Chicago in 1957, the Palazzos took part in the celebration. Twenty-five years later, in 1982, Isabella came to Valbona for my twenty-fifth anniversary as a priest and again for my fiftieth anniversary in 2007.

Giuseppe (Joe)

Joe was the oldest of the Pioli children. Although he was several years older than I, we shared much in common. We both loved sports and especially baseball. We would often play in the bocce courts in the back yard. Although Joe was a Cub fan and I was a Sox fan, this differing loyalty did not affect our relationship. Joe liked to play first base like his idol, Phil Cavaretta, and I liked to play shortstop like my idol Luke Appling. So Joe would throw me ground balls and I would whip them to first base. I had the help of a beat-up infielder's glove—compliments of the Chicago Commons.

Both Joe's idol and mine proved to be very successful. Phil Cavaretta played for the Cubs for twenty years and was the National League Most Valuable Player in 1945. However, as luck would have it, he would end his career with the White Sox in 1955.

My idol "luscious" Luke Appling, also known as "old aches and pains" would be inducted into Baseball's Hall of Fame in 1964.

Joe was kind enough to take me to Comiskey Park to see the White Sox play for the first time. It was a Sunday afternoon double-header against the New York Yankees. It was July 13, 1941. That year Joe DiMaggio would set a new major league record hitting streak of 56 games. The streak began in Comiskey Park on my birthday, May 15. We were seated in the bleachers along the right field line. I was hoping that the White Sox would snap his streak. DiMaggio would be facing my two favorite White Sox pitchers: knuckleballer Ted Lyons in the first game and lefty Thornton Lee in the second game. No such luck. DiMaggio got hits in both games and the streak continued until July 17.

Joe was married in St. Anthony's Church in Kensington where family friend Fr. Primo was stationed at the time. I was an altar boy so I served the nuptial Mass and enjoyed the reception afterwards. Joe was drafted in the Army during World War II. Unfortunately, he was killed in action on a beach in France in 1945. He left behind a disconsolate wife, Ann, and two infant children, Diane and Silvio. They would never get to know their father. My aunt Pasquina was a Gold Star Mother like so many others in those days. She hung the banner with the gold star in her front window. It was lit up at night. It was so sad to walk through the neighborhood and see so many gold stars in the window.

Joe's body was brought for burial to the cemetery in the town of Cerageto in Garfagnana in the plots reserved for the Suffredini family. In my trips to see my relatives in Valbona, I would often go to visit him in the cemetery of Cerageto which is nearby.

Dino (Don)

Don was the second child in the Pioli family. There is not much that I remember of him from my early years when we lived in the same building. Don joined the Coast Guard at a very early age. However, later in life our friendship blossomed and he became more like a brother than a cousin. Ma loved him because he showed so much kindness to her, especially after Ma was widowed. He would phone her often and always remembered her birthday.

Cousin Don Pioli singing away at my family and friends welcome home party, September 1999.

After I returned from my studies in Rome, Don was the life of the party at all of our family gatherings in Chicago. He loved the microphone and amused us with his karaoke-style singing, including songs in Italian which he had learned from his parents as a boy. He would sing and I would ham it up at the piano.

When I was stationed in Kamloops, he would come to visit me almost every year and stayed for a few weeks. He was very happy to accompany me on my trips to the Indian reservations for confirmations. He loved the Indian food, smoked salmon, moose, elk and the fried bread that the Indians called "bannock". On this bread they would spread wild honey or wild strawberry preserves. It was quite a treat.

Don was well liked by the people in Kamloops, especially the Italians. There was an Italian deli down the street from my office. In the mornings he would go there for his cappuccino and speak Italian with some of the old timers. Every year some of the folks would ask me, "Isn't your cousin coming to Kamloops this year?" Yes, of course. He hardly ever missed.

Don loved his Italian roots and his relatives in Italy. He visited them every year for over 35 years. We met up with each other in Italy several times and traveled extensively together up and down the peninsula, visiting friends and several Scalabrinian seminaries and missions.

In 1985 and again in 1990 we traveled together to Brazil to visit our relatives in the state of SãoPaulo; Santo André, San Bernardo, Riberão Pires, Campinas (where Pa was born), Brotas and Rio Claro. Our cousin Nelson Pioli and his wife Maria were gracious enough

L-R: cousins Don, Maria Pioli and husband Nelson Pioli at Vancouver's World's Fair.

to drive us south to visit the state of Rio Grande do Sul. Nelson and Maria returned our visits. They came to Vancouver in 1986 and visited the World's Fair with us. Nelson particularly enjoyed getting his World's Fair passport stamped by the various countries represented. Nelson and Maria also came to spend time with us in Kamloops. Don and I took them to a Native Indian Pow Wow. They were very impressed with the characteristic Indian clothing and the drumming competition and dancing. However, Nelson was disappointed when an Indian chief in full regalia declined to have a picture taken with him.

Not long after I retired and returned to Chicago in 1999, Don began to show signs of dementia. Over the next few years, his condition worsened and eventually he was diagnosed with Alzheimer's disease. He no longer recognized any of this children or grandchildren and no longer spoke to anyone. He was placed in a special unit in a nursing facility near Lake Forest where one of his sons lived. In spite of the fact that he seemed to have lost all contact with the outside world, I wanted so badly to go and visit him. I did so on August 16, 2008. When I entered the building, there he was, seated in his wheelchair, very well dressed, with his head bowed low and eyes closed. I spoke to him but got no response. Then I remembered what I was told by a health care worker: that people in his condition sometimes revert back to their first language and early childhood memories. So after giving him the anointing of the sick, I decided to speak to him in Italian. I recalled the good times we spent together. Suddenly his eyes opened—he looked at me and began to move his lips as though he wanted to say something to me. I was so moved by this because I was convinced that he recognized me. He passed away a few months later. I performed his funeral. There I read a poem that he had sent to me several years before. It is entitled "Dear Friend, I Remember You". It read:

If I could go back in time
Back to yesterday
We'd share secrets once again
And plan each special day

In snow and sun and rainbows
Those days of you and me
Lovely times God blessed
a friendship meant to be
Dear friend,
I love and thank you
For precious memories true
When I remember yesterday
I remember
You.

Mabel

The third and last of the Pioli children was Amabile, the name of her grandmother. This name was later changed to Mabel (Mae). On my vacation from studies in Rome, it was my pleasure to visit Grandma Amabile Suffredini. She lived in a house high up a mountain called *Il Prunaccio*. I used to spend a few days of my summer vacation in her home with my cousin Genoveffa and family. Every evening after dinner Amabile asked me to accompany her to her favorite "mestaina" where we would recite the Rosary. She was a very pious lady. The name "mestaina" is the general name given to wayside shrines, which are a familiar sight along the roads in the Garfagnana. One summer while I was visiting there with my mother, dear Amabile passed away. I was pleased to attend her funeral also on behalf of her family in Chicago.

Young Mabel and I got along very well as youngsters, even though she was a few years older than I. We would take the Chicago Avenue streetcar to go shopping at Goldblatt's, the preferred retail store of both our families, especially the basement with all its bargains. There was no Marshall Field's or Carson Pirie Scott for us. If it wasn't at Goldblatt's or Maxwell Street, it might be available from Montgomery Ward's via the catalogue. After shopping we would sometimes go to a movie at the Hub or Alvin Theaters on Chicago Avenue.

One day I told Mae that I would soon be leaving home to enter the Scalabrinian residential Seminary of the Sacred Heart in Melrose Park. She said to me: "Renzo, you are so spoiled you won't last three weeks in the seminary away from home." I guess she was just trying to test my determination. In fact, Mae would often come to see me at the seminary on visiting Sunday. Her prediction truly missed the mark. As a student and later as a teacher, I lasted in the seminary twenty-eight years. Years later, many times Mae and I laughed about her comment.

Mae married Ray Pieroni in 1951 while I was still in the

seminary in New York. They had three children, Renée, Denise, and Raymond Jr. As a priest I was happy to celebrate their twenty-fifth wedding anniversary with a Mass in their home in McHenry on January 13, 1976. Later, as bishop I was pleased to celebrate their fiftieth anniversary in their local parish church in 2001.

In 1996 Mae and her husband Ray and two grandchildren came to visit me in Kamloops. They loved the Shrine of the Immaculate Heart of Mary in Cache Creek, and we spent a few days together there. The statue of Our Lady was carved in Italy of one solid piece of lindenwood. It was donated to the shrine in honor of my parents.

Cousins Don, Mae and Ray Pieroni in the chapel of the Shrine of the Immaculate Heart of Mary in Cache Creek.

Early in 2004, Mae contracted cancer. I called her frequently because I sensed that the illness was progressing. Once I told her I would come to visit her on the following Tuesday and I would like to say Mass in the home for her and the family. She was delighted to hear that and eagerly awaited my visit.

However, on the Monday evening before my scheduled visit, I received a call from her daughter Renée telling me that Mae had lapsed into a coma and did not appear to come out of it. She wondered if it were worthwhile for me to come for the visit as planned. I said I was coming by all means—a promise is a promise. When I arrived the next morning, she was still in a coma. When I began, speaking to her, she opened her eyes. She knew exactly who I was and why I was there—much to the amazement of her children. I anointed her and then I set up a table next to her bed for the celebration of Mass. When I began, she struggled to make the Sign of the Cross and followed the Mass intently. She received the Holy Viaticum during Mass. I visited with her for a while and prayed for her. She lapsed into a coma again and died the next morning. I said the funeral Mass in the same church in which I had celebrated her 50th anniversary of marriage just a few years before. What a joy and extraordinary gift of God to be a priest and to be able to minister to those you love in their last days on earth.

I hope and pray that many young men will come to realize how much comfort the presence of a priest can give to a dying person and to the grieving family—especially one's own family. It reinforces a priest's appreciation and love for the gift of Holy Orders.

Much study is
a weariness of
the flesh.

(Ecc 12:12)

MY desire to be a priest like the three Scalabrinians in our parish was slowly maturing within me. At the same time, however, I had a difficult time giving up the idea of becoming a football player at Notre Dame like Angelo Bertelli and later with the Chicago Bears like Sid Luckman, who in 1940 led the Bears to the championship against the Washington Redskins 73–0. As a boy I listened attentively to the game on our one radio. My family did not mind because they knew my passion for football. Since there was no TV or replays in those days, I drew a football field on a piece of cardboard and charted every play. Did I like football? I prayed for a solution to this anxiety-ridden dilemma. The Lord was saying to me loud and clear "priesthood". And I kept saying "football". The controversy waged for some time. Eventually the Lord won out, and I am glad He did!

There are people in the world who try to run away from God, perhaps because they do not like what He expects of them. Francis Thompson expressed this so well in his poem "The Hound of Heaven": "I fled Him, down the nights and down the days; I fled Him down the arches of the years; I fled Him, down the labyrinthine ways of my own mind; and in the midst of tears I hid from Him, and under running laughter." But in the end, when God finally caught up with him, the author concedes: "Shade of His hand, outstretched caressingly!" And God says to him, "Ah, fondest, blindest, weakest, I am He whom thou seekest."

On September 4, 1943, at the age of thirteen, God caught up with me. I took the plunge and entered the Scalabrinian residential minor Seminary of the Sacred Heart in Melrose Park, Illinois. Today the building and property are called "Casa Italia," and is the focal point of many groups of Italian Americans of Chicagoland. It houses the Italian Cultural Center.

Some people say that age thirteen is an awfully early age to leave home and the security of the family. Maybe so. But I didn't think so. I thought of Bl. Don Guanella, Founder of the Daughters of St. Mary of Providence (DSMP) who entered the seminary at age twelve and Bl. John Baptist Scalabrini, who entered at age seventeen. By the time they entered, they surely had their minds made up. Both of them made out okay without any psychological hang-ups. However, in the Diocese of Kamloops, I ordained two men in their sixties. They too also made out very well as priests. So it seems that God calls men to His service at whatever age He pleases. I am very happy that He called me early in life. It gave me more time to learn and practice virtues that would be important in my life as a missionary.

The facility at Sacred Heart Seminary was not entirely unfamiliar to me. Fr. Primo had taken some of us altar boys to visit the Seminary. A seminarian was there to greet us and give us a guided tour of the place. He showed us the chapel, the dining room, the classrooms, the study hall, the dormitories, the bowling alleys, the ball field, etc. It sounded like a pretty nice place to me but I would quickly learn that in the minor seminary such pleasures were anything but minor. There was a strong emphasis on prayer and study. But as we read in the Scriptures, much study can be wearisome.

The bell rang very early in the morning and everyone had to be in chapel for morning prayer, a period of private meditation followed by morning Mass. I had a problem with the meditation. When the Rector, Fr. Armando Pierini, noticed that I would sleep the whole time, he ordered me and a few others with a similar problem to make the meditation while walking along the hall. After breakfast we were all assigned housekeeping chores. Eventually we were ready for morning and afternoon classes with a break for lunch. In the afternoon we made a visit to the Blessed Sacrament and had a period of spiritual reading in common. After supper we would have Rosary and Benediction of the Blessed Sacrament. The rest of the day was spent studying and doing homework. On Thursday and Sunday we did enjoy more leisure time.

For meals each of us had an assigned place in the dining room. There was no choice of foods. Everyone was served a plate of food and you were expected to finish everything on the plate with no possibility of seconds. If you left anything on the plate, you would find it at your place for breakfast in the morning. After some time we learned how to like almost everything. However, some found a way to dispose of the disliked leftovers. We had a large pond on the property where we used to play hockey in the winter. The green substances you saw on the pond were not always only algae.

Silence was a big factor in seminary life. All meals were eaten in silence as we listened to the reading of some book selected by the

Rector. There was absolute silence from after night prayer till after breakfast the next morning. This was called the "grand silence" and we had better not mess with that.

We had an annual spiritual retreat and weekly opportunities for confession and spiritual direction. On the Thursday preceding the first Friday of each month, we were all expected to make a nocturnal hour of adoration in the chapel in honor of the Sacred Heart of Jesus. As an active teenager, I cherished my sleep. The middle of the night was not my preferred time for prayer. I do much better in the morning. I learned very early in life the meaning of the term "sleep deprivation".

In a sense we were cut off from the outside world. There was no leaving the campus except for emergencies or for a walk as a group. There were no newspapers and the use of a radio was not permitted. We were not allowed to make phone calls or have visits even for those living in the Chicago area except for special circumstances. For example, while I was at Sacred Heart, my mother and father celebrated their twenty-fifth wedding anniversary. I was permitted to go and serve the Mass in our parish church but not to the reception afterwards. We were allowed a three-week vacation in the summer. We were permitted to write home once a week and all correspondence was subject to censorship. Talk about First Amendment rights. Parents and family members were allowed to visit us on the first Sunday of the month for two hours. Jenny came quite regularly. After a friendly greeting, she would begin her usual routine of squeezing my adolescent facial blackheads with her nail. I guess she wanted her little brother to look as attractive as nature allowed. I liked my sister Jenny, but not her attempts at cosmetic surgery.

Mom and Dad's 25th wedding anniversary.

Since World War II was in progress, I had heard about the rigors of boot camp for enlisted men. As seminarians we were exempt from the draft. Anyone suspected of being a draft dodger was immediately expelled from the seminary. But I thought that the minor seminary was in fact a Catholic version of boot camp with the Rector as the drill sergeant. Fr. Pierini was a no-nonsense man who believed in disciplining the undisciplined. During every study period there was an upperclassman who was charged with reporting to the Rector anyone who broke silence or caused any disturbance.

An entry in my diary for January 2, 1945, reads as follows: "During the study period, I was caught talking and was punished without supper—the first punishment of this kind that I got in fifteen months." (Not bad, eh?) But it wouldn't be the last. On April 4, 1945, the Rector was informed that some seminarians had shown disrespect to one of the faculty members. I did not like that teacher very much. We all thought he was a bit eccentric. He was a brilliant pianist, and I would have liked to sit nearby and watch him play. He would have none of that. He would lock himself in his room alone, and play while we were in the study hall. I know that was no excuse for my rude action, and I paid the price. The next morning at breakfast the Rector asked who were those who were guilty of this bad behavior. Like Honest Abe, I raised my hand together with two others, Dominic Biondi and Archie Rauzi, both from Chicago. The punishment? He was sending us home for a letter from our parents apologizing for our unruly behavior. If he did not receive the letter by 9:00 pm, we were told not to come back. I thought that was very scary. I arrived home at supper time. I was very embarrassed to see my family seated at table. They were obviously very shocked to see me unexpectedly and disappointed when I told them the reason. I remember my father telling me: "Renzo, if you don't want to be a priest anymore, that's okay. We will take you back home with open arms. But if you decide to go back, you had better learn to play by the rules." Armed with the letter, I returned to the seminary and the case was closed. Did I learn my lesson? Not quite yet. I was still a work in progress.

Once a month the Scalabrinian priests in the Chicago parishes would come to the seminary for a day of prayer and relaxation. They loved to bowl after lunch and we were assigned to set the pins for them—no automatic pin setters in those days. One time I missed my assignment which did not go unnoticed. I don't remember what the punishment was but it worked. I never missed another assignment. By this time I was beginning to get it. You don't mess with the code of discipline. Some people wonder why we put up with this kind of treatment. The answer is simple. I thought that if this was the price I had to pay to be a priest, I was ready to pay it. And many others did the same.

But all in all, life in the seminary was not all bad. We had a lot of fun. We had plenty of intramural ball games and bowling tournaments. We had other extracurricular activities. We had a glee club and a concert band. We had our first annual concert on February 16, 1947, at Mt. Carmel Church in Melrose Park. I played the bass drum and cymbals, which were not the featured instruments in most of our concert pieces. Sometimes I would miss my cue because I was busy talking with the snare drummers John and Carmen. The director, Maestro Antonio Guggino, was not pleased and made it known. I suppose he fancied himself another Arturo Toscanini and had a low tolerance for distractions.

Fr. Pierini himself directed our choir. He was very demanding as usual. I felt that he thought he was directing the choir of the Sistine Chapel in Rome.

Chuck LaVerde and I formed a photo club. We built our own printer and developed our own pictures in our darkroom. The photos turned brown after a while because I suppose we were too heavy on the acid. But it was a good try.

We also had a drama club, which performed for the seminary. One year, one of the seniors directed a Christmas play. In one scene, one of the actors exited from a tent prematurely and we heard the director shout from behind the curtains: "Hey, Mack, get back into your tent." The play went downhill after that. There were no calls from Broadway.

One summer we were given a real treat. We went to a boys' camp in Minnesota for three weeks. It was great to get away from the seminary for a while. The camp was near the town of Eveleth where the Scalabrinian Fathers administered Resurrection Church. During our stay there the pastor and the people were very good to us, providing dinner and entertainment on some evenings.

The town was not far from Hibbing, Minnesota where the Hull-Rust Mahoning Mine is located. This is the largest open pit iron mine in the world. This mine supplied as much as one fourth of the iron ore mined in the United States during World Wars I and II. The pit is more than three miles long, two miles wide and 335 feet deep. It is quite a spectacle. This was the first time in my life that I saw portions of a main road paved with iron.

Our camp was near one of the many thousands of lakes in Minnesota. We had swimming, boating, hiking and fishing. Fishing was not my idea of a sport. Holding a pole in your hand on a boat for hours without much success was not for me. I contributed nothing to the evening fish fries. Besides, I was a bit squeamish. I did not like baiting the hook with squirming worms. However, I did enjoy the campfires and the cool nights.

As I think back on those five years in the minor Seminary, I learned to appreciate the person of our Rector, Fr. A. Pierini, even though he did not seem to possess a very keen sense of humor. One day I tried to joke with him and lighten him up a bit. Holding back what might have been a smile and with a bad choice of words, he said: "Sometimes I feel like killing you." He was stunned when I answered him and said: "In the gospel Jesus

Priests and students at Sacred Heart Seminary in Melrose Park.

said: 'Do not fear those who kill the body and after that can do nothing more. But I will warn you whom to fear: fear him who, after he has killed, has authority to cast into hell." (Lk. 12:5) Studying religion came in handy. After that our relationship improved.

I can never forget Fr. Pierini and his impact on my life. He was a very holy man who practiced what he preached. He was a very private and prayerful person who spent hours at night in the chapel. No one was allowed to enter his private room. It was said that he had no bed. He slept on the floor. He washed his own clothes. He was the one who spearheaded the foundation of Villa Scalabrini in Northlake. He was also founder and editor of the newspaper *Fra Noi* (Among Us), which still has a wide circulation in the Chicagoland area. He had a weekly radio program in Italian that was very popular. He was a great devotee of the Sacred Heart and a promoter of the enthronement of the picture of the Sacred Heart in Catholic homes. In fact, on July 19, 1946, the picture of the Sacred Heart was enthroned in the living room of the Sabatini home on Erie Street.

Whenever I visited Chicago from Canada, I always made it a point to visit Fr. Pierini at Villa Scalabrini, where he resided the last years of his life. His deep spiritual life and authentic teaching influenced me in a profound way, even though I questioned some of his pedagogical methods. He would never have made Dr. Spock's top ten list, but he made mine.

After graduating from the high school seminary, twelve of us were approved for the novitiate in the Scalabrinian Congregation in Staten Island, New York. We were the first class to make our novitiate in the new St. Charles Novitiate on Flagg Place. Staten Island (Richmond) is one of the five boroughs of New York City, the others being Brooklyn, Queens, Manhattan and the Bronx. The Provincial of the New York Province, Fr. Remigio Pigato, c.s. had bought the beautiful Flagg Estate overlooking the Atlantic. This was to be the site of the novitiate and later also college and theology.

We began our novitiate on September 7, 1948, with a ceremony in our chapel. During the service we were invested with cassocks and birettas that we proudly wore every day. Our Novice Master was the kind and gentle Fr. Hector Ansaldi. He was quite a contrast from Fr. Pierini but, like Fr. Pierini, he was to have a profound impact on my life.

The year of novitiate was a welcome pause from our academic studies. The year was devoted principally to the study of the life of the Founder, Bishop Scalabrini, and the history of the Congregation. There

Fr. Hector Ansaldi, c.s. and his Novitiate Class of 1948–1949.

were a series of conferences on the Constitutions of the community and the vows of poverty, chastity and obedience. If we were deemed ready at the end of the year, we would be called to make our first temporary profession of vows. Perpetual vows would take place three years later, at which ceremony we would be given our missionary cross. I made my perpetual profession on October 5, 1952, in the Motherhouse of Piacenza in Italy.

Life in the novitiate was quite serene and peaceful in part because of the charism of our Novice Master. He was always kind and compassionate. Here is one example. One day two men drove to the seminary from Canada with a truckload of maple syrup. They had run out of money so they asked if Father Master would please buy some of the syrup. Father had pity on those poor men and bought gallons of maple syrup produced in Quebec—the real stuff. We were thrilled by his act of kindness. We could now have a breakfast of pancakes and waffles, which we rarely had before.

While the novitiate was generally a quiet place, boys will be boys. Once during summer time three of us novices got into trouble. We were huge sports fans. We had no radio or newspapers so we did not know how our favorite baseball teams were doing. We knew that the Novice Master every day received the *New York Times* which he kept in his room. We concocted a plan. John Corrao, the boldest of the three, volunteered to snatch the paper when we thought the coast was clear. John succeeded. So we sat in the shade of a large tree and began to read the sports section. We were enjoying the moment when, lo and behold, who shows up? You guessed it—the Novice Master. We were caught red-handed with no acceptable excuse. As kind as the Master was, he would not allow such a breach of discipline to go unpunished. He banned us from the annual summer picnic and we had to remain at home, weeding the garden and watering the plants. Naturally we were disappointed knowing how the rest of the class was enjoying the Staten Island beach and the evening barbeque. Did the punishment fit the crime? You make the call.

One of the saddest days of my life occurred on October 1, 1948—three weeks into the novitiate year. The Novice Master informed me that my father passed away in Italy. I was devastated because I was very close to my father. I was permitted to go home to Chicago for a memorial Mass and spend a few days with my grieving family. After the Mass I began to struggle with the idea of whether or not I should return to the novitiate or stay home and give support to my mother. She sensed my dilemma and I shall never forget the words she said to me: "Renzo, if you feel in your heart that God is calling you to be a priest, then do what He is asking of you. Don't worry about me and the family. God will look after us." After praying for enlightenment, I chose to return to New York. My mother was right. God looked after the family very well.

I appreciated so much the holiness of life of Fr. Ansaldi. He had a very strong devotion to the Blessed Virgin Mary and was a great role model for any priest. Even after we left the novitiate, he continued to follow our steps to the priesthood with an occasional letter and words of encouragement. Out of deep respect I invited him to preach at my First Solemn High Mass as a priest in the town of Valbona in 1957.

Later on in life Fr. Ansaldi was assigned to serve at the beautiful Scalabrinian parish in Milan, La Madonna del Carmine, close to the famous Duomo of Milan and La Scala Opera House. He was dearly loved by the people. In my frequent visits to Rome, I always made it a point to spend a few days with him in Milan. I was honored to be asked to preach at his 65th anniversary of ordination to the priesthood in Milan on Sunday, June 24, 2001, and again on June 28 in the Shrine of Our Blessed Mother in Rivergaro (Piacenza). Fr. Ansaldi was very devoted to that Shrine, which was not far from his home town. This shrine was also a favorite of Bishop Scalabrini. Towards the end of his life Fr. Ansaldi went to the Scalabrinian nursing home in Arco (Trento). I made a point to visit him there. It was there that he later passed away in his nineties.

When the year of novitiate was nearing the end, we were all thankfully approved to make our first religious profession of poverty, chastity and obedience. Our profession took place on September 8, 1949, the feast of the Birthday of the Blessed Virgin Mary. This was a very significant day in my life, and I placed my religious life in the hands of Our Lady. The day was special because my mother and my little sister Olga, now eighteen years of age and prettier than ever, were present at this solemn ceremony. They were so proud to see me wearing a cassock. I did not have a cassock as a boy, when she served my Mass in her room. Again, some may comment that nineteen is too young to make such a commitment. Not so. My father married when he was nineteen years old.

Upon completion of the year of novitiate, we remained in the seminary to pursue our college studies. The emphasis was on scholastic philosophy, Latin, Greek, and liberal arts.

Living in New York allowed us college students special educational opportunities. For example, our professor of English Literature took our class to Manhattan to see such Shakespearean plays as *Richard III*, with Richard Burton playing the key role, and *King Lear* with Louie Calhoun. The performances were exceptional but our assigned essays after the show were not so.

Msgr. Sheen (later bishop) and a group of seminarians after Lenten service.

One of my idols was Monsignor Fulton Sheen (later a bishop) who was a noted speaker and radio and TV personality. While we were in college, all of us seminarians went to hear his Lenten sermon in St. Peter's church on Staten Island. We were thrilled when he spent time with us after the service.

During those college days in New York, I went for organ lessons from the organist of a church in Manhattan. After several months we both agreed that Bach's preludes and fugues were not my thing. I quit taking lessons and concentrated on piano.

Since my minor seminary days, I had acquired an interest in music, especially Gregorian chant. In the summer of 1951, my friend Sandy Titta and I applied for a course in Gregorian Chant at Manhattanville College of the Sacred Heart in the city. Later the college was moved to the suburb of Purchase, New York. Sandy was ordained a priest and became quite accomplished in music and composition. He was also a highly respected parish priest.

My training in Gregorian chant came to an end after one semester when my superiors decided to send me to Rome to continue my studies toward the priesthood. Unfortunately, especially after Vatican II, the beautiful Gregorian chant fell into disuse in many places. But I still had the piano. In fact, later in those cold, long, dark winter nights in Kamloops, I had plenty of time to practice.

Before leaving for Rome, Mom and Joe came to visit me on Staten Island and came to see me off on the U.S.S. *Constitution*.

Our Scalabrinian students' residence in Rome was the International College of St. Charles. The students there were from Italy, Brazil and the United States. We attended the Gregorian University, just a few yards from the famous Trevi Fountain. There were over two thousand seminarians from fifty-two different countries—both diocesan students and members of religious congregations such as ours. At that time, all of the students wore distinctive colored cassocks together with the traditional Roman round felt hat. This uniform was to be worn at all times while attending class or when walking through the streets of Rome.

Mom and Joe visiting me on Staten Island in 1951.

Life at the Gregorian (or simply the "Greg" as we called it) was unique. All the professors were Jesuits from around the world. The common language of instruction was Latin. There was no vernacular spoken because there were too many different languages involved. All lectures and textbooks were in Latin, as well as all written and oral exams. Thank God for the years we

Aboard the U.S.S.* **Constitution** *en route to Italy. Standing L-R: Novice Master Fr. Hector Ansaldi, c.s. and brother Joe; Seated L-R: Mom, friends young Joe DiNicolo and his mom.

studied Latin in high school and college.

Rome was to be my home for nine years: two years for a degree in scholastic philosophy; four years for a degree in theology and three years of postgraduate work in canon law. By that time I was more than ready to return home to the United States. Before doing so, I not only tossed three coins in the Trevi Fountain but I also jettisoned my disagreeable Roman hat in the Tiber River to the tune of "Arrivederci, Roma". In all honesty, I must say that my nine years in the Eternal City were a huge blessing for me academically, spiritually and in many other ways. I lived and experienced every day the gift of the universality of the Catholic Church presided over by the Supreme Pontiff.

Upon my arrival in Italy, the first person to greet me was Aunt Pasquina's brother, Giannino. Our meeting was not without its adventure. Giannino was to meet me at the Port of Genoa. However, I decided to get off the boat in Naples and take my suitcases to Rome. Somehow he never got the message. The next day I took the train to Castelnuovo which you might say is the "capital" of the Garfagnana region. I arrived at the station in late afternoon and there was no Giannino to meet me. I asked the trainman where I could find him, because he was a teacher and well known in town. The trainman told me that he went to Genoa to pick up one of his relatives from America. That was me. Now what do I do, being a stranger in an unknown territory? It was getting late. I kept looking out over those mountains and bombed-out buildings. These were a visible sign of the effects of World War II. Now I had to devise some plan of action. Things did not look good at that point. The only saving grace was that I could speak Italian. Happily, a good samaritan couple saw this strange young man in a cassock and gave me shelter for the evening. The next morning I went to Mass in the parish church and as I was kneeling there, someone tapped me on my shoulder. I turned around. It was Giannino. He had driven the night from Genoa. Was I ever glad to see him.

Giannino was my only relative who owned an automobile. It was a very small car called "Topolino" (a small mouse). He was like an uncle to me. He drove me all around the Garfagnana in the province of Lucca. In addition, we visited beautiful cities, such as Florence and Lucca, with its unique wall surrounding the city. Many people would take their leisurely Sunday walks atop the wall. Giannino also took me to visit the city of Pisa with its historical church, baptistry and famous Tower. We climbed to the very top and viewed the whole area on a clear and sunny day. Despite their proximity the people of Pisa never liked the people of Lucca and vice versa. The hostility between these two cities dates back to the eleventh century. It is said to be the first war waged between Italian cities in the Middle Ages. The poet Dante Alighieri refers to it in his thirteenth century masterpiece of world literature *The Divine Comedy*. I like to believe that the relationship between these two cities has since improved.

Above all, Giannino was the one who drove me to so many different towns to visit my relatives but, of course, only those towns that were accessible by auto. Naturally, I was most anxious to meet all my aunts, uncles and cousins.

With Giannino in Pisa with Baptistry in the background.

Before beginning classes at the Greg in 1951, I made my long awaited visit to the town of Valbona, a very unusual place, not easy to locate on a map of Tuscany. My first visit was to the grave of my father, who passed away three years before. The cemetery was farther up the mountain from the church. Then for the first time I met my father's brother Decimo.

Uncle Decimo with the pastor of Valbona, Don Emiliani, who buried Dad.

When I first laid eyes on him, I got goose bumps. He was the spitting image of my father: light complexion, fair hair, blue eyes, the same gait, the same voice. No, he was not my father, but in all my years in Italy, he would prove to be just like a father to me. The same can be said of all my aunts and uncles. I had left a family behind in Chicago and I found a new family in the land of my parents and ancestors. I thoroughly enjoyed spending

Visiting Uncle Decimo's farm with relatives. L-R: Uncle Decimo, a friend, Aunt Celeste, to my left Aunt Anna and Aunt Florinda (another of Dad's sisters); seated below her is my Uncle Giuseppe with a friend. Some of my young cousins are in the front.

a portion of my summer vacation with them every year. They really loved me and were so proud of me. They prayed that indeed I would be the first of the Sabatini or Pioli clan to become a priest.

My mother came to visit me several times during my time in Italy. Of course, in her very first visit her burning desire was to visit the tomb of my father in the cemetery of Valbona. Afterwards she was able to meet all of our relatives in the various towns of the Garfagnana. I also spent time with Mother in Rome showing her some of the major historical and religious sites: the four major basilicas; the catacombs of St. Sebastian, St. Domitilla, St. Callistus and St. Priscilla; the Vatican Museum, including the Sistine Chapel; the monument to Victor Emmanuel (known to Americans as the "wedding cake"); the Colosseum and the Roman forum; the seven hills and the artistic fountains of Rome; Michelangelo's statue of Moses in the Church of St. Peter in Chains; the Church of Quo Vadis; the baths of Caracalla where Mom and I saw an outstanding production of Giuseppe Verdi's opera *Aïda* in the open air under a clear Roman sky. There are many more places in Rome that would interest tourists, especially students of art, history and religion.

An early highlight of my stay in Rome was to see the pope. The pope at the time was Pius XII. Fr. Primo had shown us altar boys a film of the coronation of Pope Pius XII in 1939. My chance came on October 21, 1951, just a few days after my arrival in Rome. I was so excited to see him for the first time in St. Peter's Basilica. He was so solemn and yet so humble and ascetic-looking. I was so impressed that I would go to the Vatican every chance I could just to see him.

It was such a privilege for me to be the *caudatario* of the Carmelite Cardinal, Giovanni Adeodato Piazza, at several papal functions. The *caudatario* was the cardinal's tail bearer at the time when cardinals wore long trains at solemn papal ceremonies. As tailbearer I would be vested in purple and sit at the cardinal's feet observing the pope's every move.

On October 17, 1953, all the students of the Greg had an audience in the Vatican and I was one of the lucky ones to get close to the Pope. I was moved when the Holy Father walked by and touched my missionary cross, which I had received the year before at my perpetual religious profession.

Also in 1953 an interesting thing happened. Before the beginning of the school year, all of us Scalabrinian seminarians made an annual eight-day retreat at our Motherhouse in Piacenza. It was during the retreat that on September 27, Cardinal Angelo Roncalli, Patriarch of Venice, unexpectedly walked into the chapel where we were assembled. He was passing through Piacenza and decided to stop in to say hello. He gave us a brief talk and his blessing. Little did we know at the time what would become of this stocky prelate.

Those of us studying in our Scalabrinian residence in Rome would meet him again, on November 4. This is the feast of our patron, St. Charles Borromeo. Cardinal Roncalli came to our seminary to celebrate the feast with us. He was a great devotee of St. Charles and wrote an extensive biography of this saint. He presided at Solemn Vespers in our chapel in the afternoon and gave a sermon about St. Charles. The cardinal stayed for dinner with us in our dining room and after dinner shared pleasantries with us. He was quite a humorous person. None of us would imagine that this elderly, simple, jovial and loving man would one day be elected pope.

My choir days with Fr. Pierini tweaked my interest in music. On Thursdays there was no school at the Greg. Some of us went each week for voluntary choral singing with Maestro Bartolucci, Director

Tailbearer of Cardinal Piazza in St. Peter's Basilica for the funeral of Pope Pius XII.

of the Sistine Chapel choir. He introduced us to the classical works of such masters as Palestrina, Orlando di Lasso, Tomás de Victoria, Perosi and others.

I also took some piano lessons with a Sicilian priest named Maestro Allegra. Whenever I would strike a discordant note, in characteristic fashion he would join his hands, and point them at me saying: "E che nota me fai?" (What sort of note are you playing?) I heard him say it quite often. However, he was very patient with his pupil.

In my many years as a student in Rome, I got to know and love the Romans. I found them to be generally happy-go-lucky. They were so open, uninhibited, and quite spontaneous in their speech. Whatever was in their minds came out of their mouths.

If you really wanted to understand the true Roman personality, you had to travel the buses or streetcars or trains where you could observe them in action. I remember several scenes in particular. In those days, the Roman buses had two employees—the driver in the front and the ticket seller in the rear. Passengers entered from the back of the bus and exited from the front. One day a heavily endowed lady entered and told the ticket seller that she only had a few stops to her destination. She asked him if she could please exit from the back because she would not be able to wend her way to the front in time. The ticket seller said to her in typical Roman dialect: *Segnò, non c'è pensà. C'è penso io.* In other words, "don't worry about it. I'll take care of it". When the woman arrived at her stop, the ticket seller shouted out to the driver of the bus for all to hear: *A Mariò, apri lo sportello de dietro; ha da scende una tonnellata,* i.e., "Mariò, open the back door; a ton has to get out." The woman was rightfully upset and as she was getting off she said to him: "I'll bet you think you're funny." Do you think that such an insensitive remark by the ticket seller would suggest a career as a standup comedian like Don Rickles? I doubt it.

Another time I was seated in the bus behind a man who was quietly reading his newspaper. In walked a young woman dressed in a miniskirt—more mini than skirt. The man spotted her from the corner of his eye. He lowered his newspaper, threw his arms in the air and shouted for her and all the passengers to hear: *Qui non c'è più religione,* i.e., "There is no more religion around here." In his own way he was deploring the mores of the holy city of Rome. The young woman was understandably embarrassed by such a loud and unexpected "welcome".

On another occasion I was on the bus with Fr. Gino Dalpiaz, a Scalabrinian friend of mine. The bus was very crowded. It was a cloudy and rainy day. Standing next to us was a man who looked very sullen. Fr. Gino tried to strike up a conversation to cheer him up. He said to the man: "Today is a pretty ugly day. What do you think the weather will be like tomorrow?" The man answered with a sense of annoyance: *E che sò, un barometro*? (What do you think I am, a barometer?) Go figure. So much for trying to brighten his day.

Romans take their soccer very seriously. There was always a long-standing rivalry between the two Roman teams of Lazio and Roma (something like Cubs and Sox in Chicago!) When a referee's call went against one's team, shouts of displeasure would ring out in the stadium. *Arbitro mutandone! Arbitro venduto*! "You are a referee with long underwear, who sold out!"

In Rome, whenever a public argument took place between two people, I never saw anything that resembled a fist-fight. There was very close contact, with loud shouting and a vulgar word or two and that was it. The argument was over.

Another time on the bus, there was a motorcade going by with a loud police escort. It was a day when the famous actress Gina Lollobrigida was visiting Rome. A lady on the bus said with glee: "It must be Gina." A man opened the window and looked out. He then slammed the window shut and said very disappointedly: "No, it's only the pope."

There were many more live episodes that convinced me that Romans were *molto simpatici*. Maybe that is why so few people from Rome left the city during the years of massive emigration from Italy to North and South America!

However, life in Rome also had its dark side. In the immediate post-World War II era, many Romans lived in poverty and the political situation was in turmoil. There were numerous strikes, many political parties and frequent elections. Communism was a force to deal with. The communists had their own daily newspaper called *L'Unità* (Unity) which had a large circulation. Their headquarters in Rome was on a street appropriately called *Via delle Botteghe Oscure* (the street of dark shops). We walked by their building every day to and from the Greg. The communists were not shy about their dislike for the Church, priests and seminarians. Because all of us walked the streets in our long black cassocks, many communists would call us *bagarozzi* (bed-bugs). We would sometimes hear them calling after us by that name. Of course, like good gospel people, we would turn the other cheek and go on our way. But not always. Read this one.

There was this famous saying in Rome: *prima nix, scholae vacant* (At the first snowfall, there is no school.) In my nine years in Rome, we rarely took advantage of that policy because it very hardly ever snowed. However, one winter in Rome we did have an exceptional snowfall with several inches of accumulation. Three of us Americans decided to spend the full day off from school walking through the streets in the snow which we enjoyed seeing after such a long time. Walking behind us was a group of rowdy teenagers. We heard them say: "Look at those *bagarozzi*. Let's give them a good pasting." They made snowballs and began throwing them at us. Were we going to turn the other cheek? Not this time. We quickly made some snowballs and began to retaliate. Italians are very good with their feet from playing soccer but not very good with their hands. We were outnumbered but not outmatched. Using our baseball skills, we fired away and hit our targets quite frequently. The lads were stunned by our response and quickly retreated even before we finished our ammunition. As they went away, we heard them say: *Ammapete—che preti*. (Holy cow! What priests!) When we were youngsters and were taunted, we would repeat that line: "Sticks and stones will break my bones but names will never hurt me." We were okay with the names but not with the snowballs. Maybe we weren't at that stage of spirituality where we were prepared to suffer persecution for the sake of the Lord.

Visiting my relatives every summer during harvest time was always a great joy for me. Some of our Scalabrinian seminarians in Rome had no relatives in Italy. So one summer I took two of our Brazilian confreres with me to the Garfagnana. My aunt and uncle in Valbona were happy to host them. One of them was Laurindo Guizzardi. Laurindo became Bishop of Bagè in Rio Grande do Sol and later transferred to the Diocese of Foz d'Iguaçu—the place of the famous waterfalls. We had a great time together that summer with my relatives.

One day the parish priest was away from the parish. Daily Mass and Holy Communion were very important to us so we decided to climb to the top of a nearby mountain and go to Mass at 6:00 a.m. in the Shrine dedicated to the saints Pellegrino and Biagio. Their bodies are buried in the church but their history is somewhat obscure. To get there in time for Mass we had to leave the house in the dark about four in the morning. Our guide was my teenaged cousin, Ello (Ralph) Rossi. He knew that mountain range like the back of his hand. (Ralph was later to emigrate to Chicago.) So with flashlight in hand and a knapsack on our back we trudged uphill. In those days we could not eat or drink anything before Communion so after Mass we sat atop the mountain and ate our breakfast as we viewed the valley below. Naturally our return down the mountain was less difficult.

Most of our summers as seminarians were spent in the Scalabrinian summer home in Villa Bassa (Niederdorf) in the Val Pusteria, which at one time belonged to Austria. We spent many hours mountain climbing. We picked wild strawberries and blueberries, porcini mushrooms, and best of all, edelweiss flowers which grew in rather dangerous places in the mountains. We would dry them in a book and then send them home to our relatives in the States. Those summers were unforgettable. We had some interesting soccer games. I was not as good with my feet as some of the other seminarians from Italy and Brazil, so I played goalie.

You are a priest forever according to the order of Melchizedek.

(Heb 5:6)

THERE are many steps that lead up to the ordination to the priesthood. Before the changes brought about by the Second Vatican Council, the steps were the following: tonsure, four minor orders, three major orders, the last of which was ordination to the priesthood.

The reception of tonsure marked the official entry into the clerical state and was normally received during the first year of theology. On December 19, 1953, four of us Scalabrinians received tonsure from an elderly, grey-bearded missionary bishop who was expelled from China. The rite of tonsure consisted of cutting some hair from the crown of the candidate's head. This ceremony was meant as a rite of passage from the secular world into the clerical state. We were expected to wear the tonsure or bald spot on the head always as a sign of our continuing commitment to the clerical state.

The four minor orders on the road to the priesthood at the time were: gatekeeper, lector, exorcist and acolyte. I received the first two minor orders in 1954 and the second two in 1955. I received the first major order of subdeacon in the spring of 1956 and the diaconate in the winter of 1956. The priesthood followed in the spring of 1957. This was a banner year for me and the fulfillment of my dream.

Final preparations for my ordination began after I received my chalice, which was my mom's precious gift to me. I designed it, and had my parents' gold wedding bands embedded in the chalice. It was made of silver and gold plated; in those days all chalices had to have at least the cup gold plated. The chalice also had to be consecrated by a bishop. After it was consecrated by Cardinal Piazza, I brought it to the Vatican asking if Pope Pius XII would deign to celebrate Mass with it in his private chapel. He did so on January 24, 1957, two months before my ordination.

It was quite exciting for me to have an altar set up in my room and begin practicing how to say Mass in Latin. This reminded me of the time as a young boy when I "celebrated" Mass at home with my sister Olga as server. This time it was the real dress rehearsal.

The big day finally arrived. My mother came from Chicago and my Uncle Decimo came from Valbona with his five-year-old son Giandomenico.

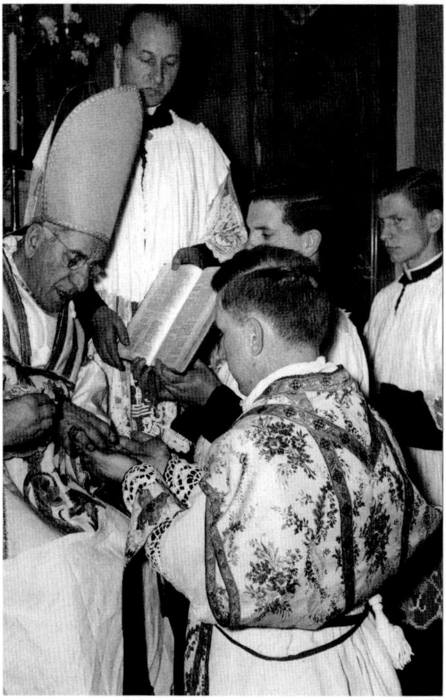

Anointing of the hands at my priestly ordination. Top left, Fr. Marco Caliaro, c.s., later bishop in Italy; to the right, acolyte Laurindo Guizzardi, c.s., later bishop in Brazil.

The ordination took place in the morning of March 19, 1957, in the chapel of our seminary. There were four of us ordained. The ordaining prelate was Cardinal Giovanni Piazza. After the ordination Mass, it is customary for the newly ordained priest to give his very first priestly blessing to his mother. I was pleased to do so. In the afternoon of my ordination I took my mom to an audience with Pope Pius XII in St. Peter's Basilica. We were close enough to greet the Pope personally. I will never forget the smile on the Pope's face when I told him that I had just been ordained a priest that very morning.

The next few days were spent celebrating Mass in my favorite holy places: on March 20, on the privileged altar of the Blessed Virgin Mary in St. Peter's Basilica; on March 21, in the Clementine Chapel below the main body of St. Peter's Basilica; on March 22, in the Borghese Chapel of the Basilica of St. Mary Major.

My first blessing as a priest to Mom.

It was on March 25 that I heard confessions for the first time, and naturally I was a bit apprehensive.

On March 30, I took the train to Castelnuovo, the main town in the Garfagnana. At that time there was no road to the town of Valbona, where I was to say my first Solemn High Mass. My Uncle Decimo picked me up in Castiglione and took me by mule to Valbona. When we arrived at the parish, the pastor, my mom, relatives, friends and a huge crowd of townsfolk were there to greet me with lit torches in their hands. While it would not want to compare myself to Jesus, it did remind me of the triumphant entry into Jerusalem. When I dismounted from the mule, the pastor took off the stole from his shoulders and placed it on mine.

I could not contain my emotion.

Communion to Mom in one of my very first Masses in Rome.

Surprisingly, during the night, a number of my relatives laid a path of fresh flowers from my mother's ancestral home where I was staying to the very door of the church. The following morning I was escorted to the church by a procession of priests and seminarians and the sound of the marching band from a nearby town. At the door of the church, I was greeted and presented with a bouquet of flowers by my little cousin Teresa. The small church was filled to capacity.

After the Mass my mom had prepared in the town square a huge barrel of wine and a mound of American-style sandwiches for the band and all the townspeople who had come to the celebration. What a treat for these wonderful people!

My mom and family and guests had dinner in the upper room of a relative's home. There Zia Maria, the best cook in town by everyone's standards, prepared a sumptuous meal that lasted almost four hours—not unusual for special Italian family dinners! The star of the show was my Uncle Decimo, and I will tell you why.

Procession to the church in Valbona for my first Solemn High Mass with Uncle Decimo to my right and Mom to my left.

Uncle Decimo had a large vineyard in his orchard and every year he would make wine. When I came to Italy in 1951, he was so proud to have a nephew studying for the priesthood that each year he would set aside the very best wine, which he bottled and stored for the banquet following my first Mass. Prior to the celebration he loaded his mule with countless bottles of his prized wine. Throughout the banquet, bottle corks were popped at frequent intervals. What is the old saying? *Vinum laetificat cor hominis*—"Wine gladdens the heart of man" (and woman).

At the celebration, my father's absence was well noted.

At the door of the church, a greeting from my cousin Teresa and presentation of a bouquet of flowers. Behind me on the far left is Fr. Angelo Calandra, c.s., former altar boy who later would succeed me as Provincial of the Province of St. John Baptist in Chicago. Immediately behind me are my Uncle Decimo and cousin Genoveffa.

The following morning I celebrated a memorial Mass for Pa in the parish church. After Mass, Mom and I and relatives went to bring flowers and pray at his grave. Pa would have been so proud to see his son as a priest.

But all good things come to an end. It was time to go back to Rome and start cramming for the written and oral comprehensive exams which marked the end of my theological studies. When the exams were over, after six years in Rome, it was time to prepare for my return to the United States. On my way, I decided to make a pilgrimage to the Shrine of Our Lady of Lourdes in France and Our Lady of Fatima in Portugal. As a boy, I had been so impressed when I saw the highly acclaimed movie *The Song of Bernadette*. What a privilege it was to celebrate a Mass at 6:00 a.m. in the grotto of Lourdes and distribute Holy Communion for an hour to the hundreds of sick and disabled people from different parts of the world. I bathed in the waters of Lourdes and took part in the very inspiring candlelight procession during which the "Ave Maria" of Lourdes was sung in many different languages.

On leaving Lourdes, I made a two-day stopover in Madrid, Spain where I celebrated Mass in the beautiful Church of San Francisco el Grande. I visited the famous Escorial and the tombs of the kings. No bullfights, please. Eventually I arrived in Fatima and spent a few days there. I said Mass in the Shrine and visited the home of Lucia, one of the three shepherd children to whom the Blessed Mother appeared. The pilgrimages to Lourdes and Fatima were more than I had anticipated and a real spiritual retreat for this newly-ordained priest.

From Fatima I went to Lisbon where I celebrated Mass in the cathedral. On July 9, I boarded the steamship *Saturnia* in Lisbon for my return to the United States. On July 17, after eight days at sea, we reached New York Harbor. What a thrill it was to see the Statue of Liberty again. One of my very first stops in New York was to buy a hot dog from one of those pushcart vendors. In Rome, there was no such thing as a good old-fashioned New York hot dog.

From there it was on to Chicago where I spent the summer with Mom and family and visited old friends. On September 22, 1957, I celebrated my first Solemn High Mass in the United States at my home parish of Santa Maria Addolorata on May and Erie Streets. Fr. Primo, long-time family friend, played a major role in the celebration. I remember well the words he spoke to me in the sacristy after Mass. He was so proud of his former altar boy. He said to me: "Renzo, you celebrated this Mass with great devotion. Celebrate the Mass every day of your life in the same way." He was even more proud of me when I was ordained bishop in 1978. By then he had retired and was back in Italy, where he died in 1980.

My sister Jenny arranged the afternoon reception in the Congress Hotel. It was not long afterwards that the wrecking ball arrived on the scene and made short work of the second Addolorata Church, the school, our home and the surrounding neighborhood.

Banquet at Congress Hotel after my first Solemn Mass in Santa Maria Addolorata Church. At head table, Fr. Primo, Mom and my chalice.

On October 7, I was on my way back to Rome to pursue graduate studies in canon law. I made one stopover in Stockholm where I said Mass in the Dominican Church of the Assumption and took a guided tour of this beautiful Swedish city. While visiting one of the churches, our guide, seeing me in clerical clothes, deplored the fact that not many Swedes use the church.

One year later, several important events took place while I was living again in our Scalabrinian residence. Cardinal Marcello Mimmi, the Archbishop of Naples, was named Prefect of the Consistorial Congregation which is the dicastery charged with researching the appointment of bishops. It is now called the Congregation of Bishops. The Cardinal came to live with us in our seminary for a few months. As a newly-ordained priest, I was honored to assist him at Mass in our chapel several times. Once he invited me to join him in his chauffeur-driven automobile for a leisurely ride in the country. I was seated next to him in the back seat of the car and was impressed to see him reading *The Imitation of Christ* by Thomas à Kempis. I had read the book in grammar school when I was preparing my "first sermon".

During that year, besides studying, I was also anxious to do some pastoral work. Each Sunday I went to the Church of Regina Pacis where I heard confessions for at least two hours.

The Sacrament of Penance is such an extraordinary gift to the Church. Jesus conferred the power to forgive sins in His name to the Apostles and their successors in the priesthood. Jesus said to the Apostles after His resurrection: "Receive the Holy Spirit. For those whose sins you forgive, they are forgiven; for those whose sins you retain, they are retained." (Jn. 20:23). The grace of the Sacrament of Penance not only remits past sins but strengthens the penitent's resolve to avoid sin and the proximate occasion of sin in the future. After more than fifty years of hearing confessions, I am still in awe of the power conferred on me in the sacred ordination. How many times I have heard people tell me after confession: "Father, I want to thank you. You have been a great help to me. I am now free of the sins that have troubled me for so long." I wonder how many times St. John Vianney must have heard similar words as he sat in the confessional, sometimes for as many as sixteen hours a day during his forty years as the Curé of Ars. He is certainly deserving of the title "Patron of Parish Priests". Every priest is not only God's agent of forgiveness but also a subject as well. For this reason, priests, bishops, cardinals and popes go to confession regularly.

When I was a student in Rome, it was well known that Pope Pius XII went to confession each week to a very learned and holy man. He was a Jesuit priest by the name of Fr. Cappello. This humble man also heard confessions in a Jesuit church every week and the line to his confessional was very long. I know because one day I lined up myself. The line was not moving very fast so I moved and went elsewhere—impatient me.

I was very fortunate to have Fr. Cappello as my professor of canon law in graduate school at the Greg. He was quite an unusual lecturer. When the bell rang for class he would begin promptly with a prayer, and he would close the class with a prayer when the dismissal bell rang. He would come into class with no book or papers. He would lecture in Latin for the whole fifty minutes. He would quote word for word from memory all the pertinent Canons of the Code of 1917 which was operative until the new Code of Canon Law of 1983.

One day one of the students brought an alarm clock to class. He thought he would trick Fr. Cappello by setting it off midway through the period. He thought that Fr. Cappello would think it was the school bell and promptly dismiss the class as he always did. No such luck. Fr. Cappello paused until the alarm stopped and then, unperturbed, he continued the lecture till the very end. In his humility, he made no issue of that failed prank.

There were many occasions to visit some of the famous places of Italy such as Naples and Sorrento and the famous city of Pompei where I celebrated Mass in the crypt. Driving the beautiful Amalfitana coast was a breathtaking experience.

During this time several of us Scalabrinians visited the Benedictine Monastery of Monte Cassino which was heavily bombed during the Second World War. The huge death toll was visible in the Polish cemetery on the grounds. It was remarkable to see how the monks restored that historical monastery to its original beauty. We also visited the town of Orvieto which is famous not only for its wine but also for its church with its magnificent façade. We took a trip to the towns of Anzio and Nettuno. Anzio has a beautiful and well-kept American cemetery where thousands of our soldiers are buried. Nearby is the town of Ferriere, which was the home of the young martyr, Santa Maria Goretti. We visited the church of Nettuno and the hospital where this martyr of purity died.

In May of 1958, Cardinal Stritch passed away. He was the former Archbishop of Chicago and an official of the Vatican. Cardinal Mimmi invited me to be his *caudatario* (tailbearer) at Cardinal Stritch's funeral in the Church of St. Ignatius.

I spent the summer of 1958 in Switzerland where I had hoped to learn German. I stayed at the Italian Catholic Mission in Basel which was under the care of the Scalabrinian Fathers. It was in Basel that I performed my very first nuptial (wedding) Mass. The groom was an Italian immigrant worker and the bride was a Swiss girl.

During that summer I also visited the capital of Bern and the city of Geneva where I met some of my cousins who had emigrated there from Italy several years before.

On October 9, 1958, shortly after my return to Rome, my idol Pope Pius XII passed away in his summer villa at Castelgandolfo. I went there to pay my respects. I also took part in the procession when the body of the late pope was transferred from the Basilica of St. John Lateran—the pope's Cathedral Church—to St. Peter's Basilica.

Once again I was privileged to be the *caudatario* of Cardinal

Mimmi, who pontificated at the final funeral Mass for Pope Pius XII in the presence of thirty-five cardinals. As I was in the sacristy after the Mass helping Cardinal Mimmi divest, I could not help looking at those thirty-five cardinals and wondering which, if any, would be the next pope. I saw Cardinal Roncalli seated there and, even though I remembered his visits to us Scalabrinians and what a good man he seemed to be, I said to myself: "It can't be him. He is so different from the late pope and to me he just would not look right wearing the papal tiara." Little did I know.

When the conclave to elect the new Pope was convened, school notwithstanding, I made sure to be in St. Peter's Square twice a day to watch the smoke emanate from the Sistine Chapel where the cardinal electors were in session. For a few days, the smoke was black, meaning the new pope was not yet elected. Finally, at 5:00 p.m. on October 28, the smoke was white. Suddenly the whole square was filled with several hundred thousand people curious to see who the next pope would be. Finally the Cardinal Chamberlain appeared on the balcony of the Basilica and made the customary announcement: *Habemus Papam*, i.e., "We have a pope. His name is Angelo." Before he could complete the sentence, I jumped with joy as I knew that there was no other Cardinal named Angelo except Roncalli. He took the name of John XXIII. I could not believe it: this was the man who had visited us twice. On Christmas morning I went to St. Peter's Basilica to attend Pope John's first Christmas Mass.

Audience with Pope John XXIII. Upper right with Ed Moretti.

One of the twenty-three cardinals named by Pope John XXIII on December 18 was Cardinal Giuseppe Antonio Ferretto who was a friend of our Scalabrinian community. He invited some of us to join him and his family at a special audience with the pope. What an exciting experience! Pope John XXIII was his usual jovial and humorous self. With me at that audience was my friend Ed Moretti. He had served at my ordination ceremony and two years later, I would assist him at his ordination and first Mass. Later during the Vietnam War, Fr. Ed joined the Army as a chaplain. He was a highly decorated soldier, honored for bravery under fire during the Tet Offensive. After leaving the service, he became a very successful pastor and eventually Vicar General of the Diocese of Venice, Florida.

The year 1958 ended with a visit to the town of Rieti not far from Rome. This was the See of Bishop Massimo Rinaldi. Rinaldi was the very first Scalabrinian ever to be named a bishop. He was a truly saintly and pastoral bishop whose cause for beatification is in progress in Rome.

The year 1959 had its highlights for me. Since I had the good fortune of having Pope Pius XII as the first one to celebrate Mass with my chalice, I hoped that Pope John XXIII would also use my chalice. He did so on the first of February. On Pentecost Sunday, May 17, once again I assisted Cardinal Mimmi in St. Peter's Basilica for Solemn Vespers which were presided over by Pope John XXIII. In the evening of Sunday, June 28, I was once again in St. Peter's with Cardinal Mimmi for the first Vespers of the Solemnity of St. Peter in the presence of the pope.

It was always a joy for me to welcome my mom on her visits to Rome. She was particularly thrilled on August 19 to go to Castelgandolfo for a papal audience with Pope John XXIII. My mom grew to have a loving devotion to "good Pope John," who one day might be declared a saint.

On Sunday, December 6, it was a thrill for us Americans in Rome to greet President Dwight Eisenhower in St. Peter's Square on his way to an audience with Pope John XXIII. President Eisenhower was visibly moved to see the enthusiastic reception of his fellow Americans and to hear the shouts of "We like Ike."

It was such a relief for me when on June 13, 1960, I completed my doctoral studies in canon law. Then all I could think about was returning home to the States after a total of nine years in the Eternal City. On my way home, I made a pilgrimage to the Shrine of Our Lady of Loreto, where I celebrated a Mass of thanksgiving for the grace of completing my studies. From there I went to Paris.

I was in Paris for their national holiday of July 14 and enjoyed the military parade and other festivities. Paris had so many famous attractions: the Eiffel Tower, the Louvre Museum, Montmartre, the Cathedral of Notre Dame, and others.

Teach them to
obey everything
I have commanded
you.

(Mt 28:20)

AFTER arriving in the States, I spent a month with family and friends before reporting to my new posting on August 22. I was assigned to teach Moral Theology and Canon Law in St. Charles Seminary on Staten Island, where I had already spent three years as a student. In addition to my classroom duties, I enjoyed weekend pastoral work in parishes on the Island.

On December 16, 1960, a tragic accident occurred that I will never forget. I was teaching class when suddenly we heard a loud explosion. One of the students looked out the window and realized that two commercial airliners had collided in mid-air just above the island. One of the two planes crashed in a small air strip called Miller Field. It was a very short distance from the seminary. Two of us priests immediately drove to the site of the crash, and on our way we saw human limbs and suitcases dangling from trees and power lines. Actually, the two of us were among the first to arrive on the scene. The fire trucks, police and ambulances arrived shortly after. We walked through the snow and saw several bodies (or parts thereof) lying in the snow, some badly burned. The smell of the charred bodies was nauseating. We saw crushed bodies being carried out of the fuselage of the plane. There were no survivors. We prayed over the bodies that we saw lying in the snow. We prayed also for their families as many of the passengers were on their way to celebrate Christmas with their loved ones. The sight and odor of that tragic scene remained with me for days.

That same evening we were invited to NBC Studio in New York for the taping of Perry Como's annual Christmas show. The tragedy of the morning cast a dark pall over that whole event. Perry Como greeted us warmly when he learned that we were priests and seminarians.

On October 4, 1965, Pope Paul VI came to New York to address the United Nations on the question of world peace. In the evening he celebrated a papal Mass in Yankee Stadium and we were happy to be present. That was the first time I saw this pope who was to play an important role in my future life.

During those years I also had the opportunity of making use of my canonical training outside the classroom. I was invited to serve on the Matrimonial Tribunal of the Archdiocese of New York in the capacity of Advocate in marriage annulment cases. This role is somewhat similar to that of an attorney for the plaintiff in civil law. The jurisprudence of the Church was developing at that time. I found the work quite interesting, and it was a pleasure to work with fellow Iona graduate Monsignor Desmond Vella, who would later become judicial vicar of New York's archdiocesan tribunal.

About the same time, Bishop George Guilfoyle, the Episcopal Vicar of Staten Island, invited me to serve as his Master of Ceremonies for confirmations in about forty parishes on the Island. In 1968 Bishop Guilfoyle was appointed diocesan bishop of Camden, New Jersey. He invited me to attend his installation. He was so proud of me when I was named a bishop ten years later. After all those confirmations with Bishop Guilfoyle, I had all the ceremonies down pat. I did not know it at the time, but the experience would serve me well in the future.

The eight years I spent teaching Scalabrinian seminarians were a joy and a privilege for me. Helping these young men appreciate their gift of priesthood and the importance of spiritual and academic formation helped me appreciate more my own vocation. I was thrilled to attend their ordinations to the priesthood. These newly-ordained priests went on to have successful ministries to migrants and refugees throughout the world. Some even became provincial superiors of their respective provinces. Another, Silvano Tomasi, became an archbishop and Vatican diplomat. Fr. Peter Polo, c.s. who for several years was Procurator and Secretary General in Rome was always very helpful to me.

During my teaching years on Staten Island, we were blessed to have good Rectors and formators. One was Fr. Joseph Visentin, c.s. He was intelligent and a good leader of both faculty and seminarians. Later he was assigned as spiritual director of the Scalabrinian seminarians in Manila. When I was in Manila for the papal visit, I went to see him in the seminary. At his age he was studying Tagalog. How's that for dedication?

Another was my novitiate classmate, Fr. Alex Dalpiaz, c.s. He served many years as a missionary in Queensland, Australia, and in Colombia. As rector, he brought his personal missionary experiences to those seminarians in formation.

Another one was Fr. John DiVito, c.s., a pious and pastoral missionary in various parts of the world. Later in life he was chaplain of Villa Scalabrini in Northlake. I was honored when he invited me to preach the homily at his fiftieth anniversary of priestly ordination in October of 1996 in St. John Vianney Church in Northlake. I came from Kamloops for this special occasion. Fr. John spent his last years at the nursing home of the Little Sisters of the Poor in Palatine. He died right after Mass on the Solemnity of the Body and Blood of Christ, to which he was greatly devoted. I was asked to preside at his funeral on June 18, 2009, in Mt. Carmel Church in Melrose Park. His interment took place in the Scalabrinian plot in Queen of Heaven cemetery in Hillside.

While teaching on Staten Island in the 60's, I had occasion to meet two interesting people. One was Judge Samuel Liebowitz. He was a well-known judge and best remembered as counsel in several notorious trials, such as the Scottsboro trial of nine African-American youths in the South who were falsely accused of raping two white women and who were sentenced to death in Alabama in 1930. Liebowitz accepted to be counsel for the defense and worked on the case pro bono for four years. He received death threats, and the National Guard was assigned to protect him. The Supreme Court reversed the decision, and Liebowitz called it "a triumph for American justice". After the case, he returned to New York and in 1962 he was named New York State Supreme Court Justice. That is when I met him. He invited me to be a guest of the court at a murder trial of two accused criminals. One of the defendants was picked up by the police in a motel outside Chicago. The judge knew I was from Chicago so he thought I might be interested. I was, because I had never been inside a criminal court before. This was the day when he would charge the jury and seek the verdict. While talking with him in his chambers before the session, I asked him if he thought the defendants were guilty. He said yes and told me to listen to what he had to say in court. Liebowitz was famous for giving a wordy presentation when charging the jury. This one was no exception. He was long and eloquent, and the jury quickly came out with a verdict of guilty. I could not help thinking about what was going through the minds of the accused when they saw this priest sitting close to the judge's bench. Bad omen?

The other person was Brian Piccolo, a running back for the Chicago Bears. In spite of all my years in New York, I always remained a loyal Bears fan. In 1969 Brian was diagnosed with malignant lung cancer. He was admitted to the Sloan-Kettering cancer clinic where he underwent an operation. I decided to go and visit him after the operation. He was happy to see this unknown priest. We prayed together. He ordered a pizza and invited me to join him. In the hallway I had met his wife Joy and their three young daughters. Brian was a truly loving and compassionate human being. It was reported that from his hospital bed he was watching the Arkansas-Texas game on December 6 when one of the Texas players was injured and taken to the hospital. His name was Fred Steinmark. He was diagnosed with malignant cancer of the left leg which had to be amputated. Brian immediately wrote him a letter in which he told him of his own operation. He told him that their lives were in the hands of God just as they were before their illnesses were discovered. He urged him to pray to God as he does for the strength to carry out the plans God laid out for them. Those are the sentiments of a true believer. Brian died on June 16, 1970 at the age of twenty-six and Steinmark died one year later. In 1971 when I was in Canada, Hollywood made a movie of the life of Brian Piccolo and his friendship with Gale Sayers, his fellow running back on the Bears. It was entitled *Brian's Song*—a very moving film.

After seeing the movie I decided to write a letter of condolences to Brian's wife Joy telling her how our parishioners in Vancouver prayed for Brian and his family. Joy was kind enough to answer my letter on February 3, 1972. This is what she wrote:

> Dear Reverend Sabatini,
>
> Thank you for writing me in such a warm and comforting way.
>
> My husband was, indeed, a wonderful man and it makes me very happy to know that he is fondly remembered by those who knew him. Even though he is no longer with us, so many people have learned to know and appreciate his unquenchable zest for life.
>
> My daughters and I will be forever grateful for what Brian gave us and for the friendship which you and so many others have offered. Thank you for remembering Brian in your sermon.
>
> Sincerely,
> Joy Piccolo

Like so many other religious communities in the late 60's, the Scalabrinians closed St. Charles Seminary in 1968. Our seminaries were sent elsewhere to consolidate with other theology students. That left me pretty much unemployed. However, I was already preparing for new ministries.

To counsel the doubtful.

(Spiritual Work of Mercy)

IN 1965, while still teaching, I had enrolled in a program of pastoral counseling at Iona College in New Rochelle, New York. I graduated with a Master's degree in 1968.

One person who came to my graduation was Fr. John Coleman. He was Mom's pastor at St. Bede's in Ingleside. He was a very interesting person. My mother was fond of him and respected him as she did every priest she met. Fr. Coleman had his own way of doing things. When I was still in the seminary and came home for vacation, Mom and I would go to church every morning and I would serve his Mass. He made it a point of letting me know how inept I was at serving Mass. If I answered the Latin prayers too loudly, he asked me if I thought he was hearing impaired. If I said them too softly he would ask me if I had laryngitis. You could never win. I guess this was his way of saying that he was happy to have me around.

My mom owned a restaurant in his parish and he was always an honored guest. He went there almost every Friday but would not enter through the main door. He went through the kitchen, just like a member of the family. He would sit on a barstool in the kitchen and order his meal. My mother felt that this was not an appropriate place for a priest to sit for dinner. So one day Mom said to him: "Father Coleman, it's very hot in this kitchen. Why

Graduation at Iona with Fr. Coleman, Mom, her daughter-in-law Virginia and Virginia's daughter Lisa.

don't you go into the air conditioned dining room? We have a table reserved for you and a waitress to look after you." He was quick to reply: "Don't tell me what to do." My mother was not offended. She knew him all too well. Beneath that gruff exterior, internally he was a warm-hearted person. Sometimes he would show this side of him. What else would have made him decide to come to my graduation on his own? My family was saddened by his death in 1973, five years before my consecration as bishop. If he had been living at the time, I'm sure he would have had some characteristically Coleman-like words of wisdom for me.

I began to do counseling in high schools and privately as well. It was then that I discovered the great need that young people had for guidance in this very stressful period in their life, especially with the proliferation of drugs, drink and other forms of unacceptable social behavior.

As part of the requirements for the degree from Iona, I was assigned to do field work at the Staten Island Mental Health Clinic under the supervision of the psychiatrist director, Dr. Silberstein. Being a priest, the matter of the dress code came up while I was at work in the clinic. The director left it completely up to me whether I wanted to dress in a clerical suit or in civilian clothes. I preferred to dress in priestly attire. The director pointed out that if this should present a problem for some client, I would have to deal with it. I was prepared to accept the challenge.

In fact, one day, a client who was assigned to me arrived and sat in the waiting room. The receptionist phoned my office upstairs and said that my client was here for his appointment. When I came down to meet him dressed as a priest and introduced myself as "Father Sabatini", I could see the look of shock and disappointment in his eyes. He probably felt that he would be given a stern lecture about God and religion. However, he did agree to come up to my office for the initial interview and social intake.

In the beginning he was less than cooperative, and his answers were curt. I tried very hard to establish a working relationship with him but, towards the end of the interview, I had to confront the issue. I told him that I felt he was uncomfortable speaking to a priest in a public clinic. He quickly opened up and animatedly told me that once he went to a Catholic church and heard the priest preaching about something which offended him. He vowed never again to go to church or have anything to do with priests. This man was a high school teacher who had bad experiences with women. He was divorced, with two teenage daughters who were causing him serious stress. I told him that I understood his feelings and to help him I would ask the Director to assign him another counselor. He thought about it for a while and then said: "No, thanks. With my luck, he might assign me a woman counselor. I'll stick with you. You seem to be an O.K. guy." What's the old saying? "The habit doesn't make the monk."

After my graduation from Iona, the idea of doing more to help troubled young people continued to haunt me. I spoke about this to my friend Sam Panepinto. Sam was a veteran of World War II and was wounded in action. He suffered spinal cord injury which confined him to a wheelchair for the rest of his life. In spite of his disability, he was one of the most energetic and dynamic people I have ever met. He was involved in his church and was successful in working with youth. Sam was very interested in my idea, and he promised to help me in every possible way. We talked about the possibility of opening up in a storefront for youth counseling. We visited various possible sites. We needed seed money to begin the project. Sam had connections with local politicians and business people of the community. They all agreed to help. No one would ever say "no" to Sam. He was always so persuasive, and everyone trusted his honesty and integrity. The center was about to become a reality in a store front on New Dorp Lane.

On June 1, 1970, the local newspaper, the *Staten Island Advance* announced the opening of the new youth center. Funding for the project came from the City and State of New York as well as from grants and other private contributions. The legal title was Young People's Information Service (YPIS). The young people referred to it as RAP center (Relief Against Problems). The center was open free of charge to anyone who wanted to "rap" (talk) in a very confidential and informal way with someone who cared. We were able to assemble a good staff. The center was open after school hours from 3:00 to 10:00 p.m. All the pieces were in place and final government approval was given on September 21, 1970. The official opening of phase one was an open house on Sunday, October 15, 1970. Phase two opened on May 16, 1971.

After my departure from New York in the summer of 1971, Sam took over full responsibility for the center. Under his leadership, from a small seed it grew into a huge tree. Today it is called the New York Center for Interpersonal Development (NYCID) with a staff of 145 people and a budget of over three million dollars. This sum is provided through grants from the City and State of New York. They also have numerous offices in a rent-free city building in St. George, Staten Island. Quite a substantial development from the little storefront on New Dorp Lane.

It is inspiring to meet and work with people who are totally and unselfishly dedicated to the wellbeing of their fellow men and women.

During the time of my involvement with RAP and with the high schools, I worked with a large number of teenagers. Some were able to overcome their problems. Others were not. I was deeply saddened whenever I was not able to point their lives in a more positive direction. Let me share with you the stories of five people who come to mind.

Michelle

Michelle was a senior who attended one of my courses on marriage in her Catholic high school. She appeared to be totally disinterested in what I had to say and would not participate in any of the discussions. She spent much of the time looking out the window. She was a tall, attractive and very intelligent young lady. She was awarded a scholarship to one of the more prestigious colleges in New York City.

After her graduation, I never expected to see or hear from her again. However, about a year after graduation, I received a phone call from someone who said: "Hi, Father. My name is Michelle. Remember me? I was in your class last year as a senior." I thought to myself: "No, it can't be that Michelle." But it was. She said: "I would like to speak to you because I enjoyed your classes and I feel that you are the only one I can really talk to." And again I thought: "You surely had me fooled."

When she came to see me, I noticed that her left wrist was bandaged. Then she told me her story. She came from a dysfunctional family. She was depressed and totally disgusted with life. One night she wanted to take her life and slit her wrist with a razor. By chance, her mother walked into her room and found her unconscious in a pool of blood. She was rushed to the hospital and the doctors were able to save her life. She came to see me to voice her extreme anger at her mother for finding her in that state when she really wanted to end it all. We talked for a long time. My immediate goal was to motivate her to see a psychiatrist with whom I had worked in the Staten Island Mental Health Clinic. She would not do so. I offered to see her on a regular basis but she never returned. I was not able to gather any information about her after I left the Island. Is she alive, or did she try to take her life a second time? I don't know. But I have long agonized over her. She was a gifted person with a potentially bright future ahead of her. May the Lord look after her wherever she is.

Billy

While teaching high school religion in a school for boys, I had one boy in the junior class who was a model student. His name was Billy. He was polite, interested in school, and well liked by all his classmates. He loved basketball but was too short to make the team. The team members voted him their manager. He would sit on the team bench at every game. He provided water and towels and a word of encouragement to all the players. It was a huge blow to everyone when Billy was diagnosed with cancer. One leg had to be amputated. After the operation, I went to see him in the hospital. Before going into his room, I was praying and wondering what I could say to a young man in his condition. When I walked in, he greeted me with his usual smile. His positive attitude put me at ease. He was that kind of person.

Billy wanted to return to school as soon as he was able. He would come to class on crutches. Everyone was so happy to see him. He returned to his assignment as manager of the basketball team. The players might have said: "Let's win one for Billy", just as Knute Rockne had told his players: "Win one for the Gipper." They went on to win the championship that year.

During the summer of 1970, Billy passed away. The vigil service and the funeral Mass were crowded with people, especially teenagers and students of the school. There was not a dry eye among them. They had all lost a positive role model and a dear friend.

Billy never made it to his graduation the following year. At the commencement exercises, the salutatorian dedicated the graduation ceremony in memory of Billy. This elicited a standing ovation from the large crowd of students and their families. Billy was gone, but he was definitely not forgotten.

Patrick

When Patrick was a young boy, he lost his mom in a fire that destroyed their home. His father tried his best to raise the boy, but Patrick missed his mom very much. When Patrick entered high school he was doing very well until he fell in with the wrong crowd. At the age of fifteen he began to experiment with drugs, and before long he was injecting himself with seven or eight bags of heroin a day. He boasted to me that he was the third best "junkie" in New York. He was soon expelled from school. He and his drug-taking friends would go to an abandoned shack on one of the Staten Island beaches and spend weekends getting high on drugs. Patrick was always the provider. He would forge checks to buy drugs. The group would steal from delivery trucks the food they needed to survive.

Patrick would come to see me at RAP from time to time to talk about his problems. When I hadn't seen him for a while, I decided to go look for him. I found him in the back of a warehouse. There he was, sitting in a fetal position, perspiring and shaking uncontrollably. He was having a severe withdrawal. I spent some time with him and offered to get him into a residential facility where he would be helped with the withdrawal. He did not agree. He told me that he wanted to conquer his habit by himself. Unfortunately, he could not. He was arrested by the police and had to appear in court. I pleaded with the judge not to send him to Riker's Island where I felt that he might turn into a hardened criminal. The judge, who happened to be a member of the board of directors of RAP, agreed with me. He put Patrick on probation with the condition that he come in to see me at RAP on a regular basis. Patrick was quite cooperative and appeared to be heading in the right direction. In July of 1971, I left Staten Island for a new assignment in British Columbia. Patrick was not happy to see me go. He may have considered my departure as another rejection in his life. He got deeper and deeper into the drug scene. Later on he was arrested again and, unfortunately, this time he was sent to Riker's Island.

A month after I left, I received word that Patrick took his life inside Riker's Island four days before his twenty-first birthday. Patrick has been on my mind all these years.

Patty

Patty had a twin sister named Dee. They both attended the same girls' high school where I was counselor. Both attended my weekly group counseling session with three or four other girls. These girls were very disruptive in the school and the principal wanted to expel them. I pleaded with her to let me try to help them make it to graduation. Happily, they did.

Dee was the ringleader of the group. Her sister Patty was extremely protective of her twin. Of course, Dee took full advantage of this. While Patty attended the weekly sessions, I believe her only purpose was to keep a watchful eye on her sister.

Patty's personality was so much different from that of Dee. Patty was a non-aggressive, kind and caring young lady. She was very helpful to us in setting up the RAP center. She was so proud to be hostess at the official opening of the center.

It was not long after her graduation that I was transferred to British Columbia. Patty was saddened by this because she confided fully in me. She always referred to me as "big brother" and called me "Sabby". She wrote to me regularly and I would answer her almost immediately because I detected a cry for help in her letters.

Two years or so after graduating high school, she took up with a drug addict. I suspect she did so to help him get off drugs. But the opposite happened. She became addicted. The two of them went to a deserted area in upstate New York and lived the life of so-called "hippies". They went fishing and hunting with bows and arrows. They spent most of their days getting high on drugs. Then one day I received the following letter from her dated May 23, 1973:

> Dear Sabby,
>
> Hi—
>
> I know I haven't written and I am sorry but . . .
>
> I started writing you letters many times but it didn't sound like I should sound so I gave up. This will be mailed even if it doesn't sound like me.
>
> I've had my head pretty messed up—the reason I still can't talk about, it hurt so much. But it's pretty bad. I'm gonna be very honest about its effect on me so prepare yourself. First—I am a head now—I do anything from Pot to Mes. with a variety of other pills in between. I haven't had too many days in which I was straight for quite some time. In fact I had an accident.
>
> Second—Sexual Freedom not complete freedom but times of weakness have been part of my recent life. I spent one weekend in a motel in the Bronx. I don't think I need go any further in that aspect.
>
> Third—I am fXXXed-up. My head is constantly spinning—my nerves are shot. I go into fits of severe depression and cry uncontrollably. At times I have almost thrown myself down stairs or in front of cars—but always stop. One of these times [I won't]. I feel so alone and isolated, so apart from all as if I weren't real, and life was a pitiful nightmare.
>
> I'm trying to solve all this but it involves someone else who may not be so willing. And the funny part is I couldn't care less about what happens to me—
>
> In any case—don't be too surprised if you hear something happened to me. Or I disappeared.

Please have a wonderful celebration for your birthday.
Much Love Always,
Pat
P.S. Write soon, Big Brother. I need you now.
Sis

I answered the letter immediately, recognizing the urgency of the situation. But I never received another letter. On every visit to New York, I tried to track her down but to no avail. She seemed to have left planet Earth. Is she alive or did she carry out her threat? No one knows for sure. I trust that if she were still alive, she would have kept in touch with her "big brother". I mourn the fact that I was not around when she needed me most.

Maryann

One day in 1970 two young girls from a Catholic girls' high school came to visit me at RAP. One of them was Maryann. She had heard about our storefront youth counseling center and decided to check it out. Initially the two of them would come together. Later she told me she did this to test whether I was the kind of person she felt comfortable enough to speak with. When she felt that she could trust me, she came for counseling alone. Her story was that her mother was an alcoholic who physically and emotionally abused her since she was an infant. By the age of eight she had already decided that eventually she was going to run away from home. As a teen she became very rebellious. While at school she would smoke cigarettes, pot, take drugs, drink and break the school dress code. She was a very troubled young lady. Our counseling relationship was terminated prematurely when I was assigned to Canada.

She kept in touch with me with an occasional letter or phone call. Her situation at home was becoming more and more intolerable. But she was able to survive and made it to graduation. She was a very intelligent young lady and graduated easily without opening up a book very often. After I was gone, Maryann continued to go to RAP to speak to my friend and co-founder Sam Panepinto. She trusted him and liked him. Sam was hospitalized for two years in the Veterans' Hospital in the Bronx for treatment related to his spinal cord injury. During that time, I decided to go to New York to visit him. Maryann had kept in touch with him, so the two of us drove to the hospital where we visited with Sam for several hours.

On Sunday, June 7, 2009, I was invited to Staten Island to preach at the fiftieth anniversary Mass of a priest confrere of mine. Guess who was present at the Mass? Maryann. I was so happy to see her. Before my return to Chicago, Sam and I decided for old times' sake to take her out for dinner at her favorite restaurant. During the meal we had an interesting conversation, one which I will never forget.

Maryann asked me if I remembered a conversation we had on the Staten Island Ferry in the spring of 1971. I had no recollection of such a meeting. Then with tears in her eyes she began to tell me what happened that day. She finally decided to leave home as she said she would at eight years of age. She packed her bag and took off. But she had nowhere to go. So she decided to stay on the ferry, going back and forth across the bay and sleeping on the ferry as well. Then one day she saw me and my mother board the ferry. I remembered that my mother did come to New York to visit me that year, and I did take her on the ferry so that she could see close at hand the Statue of Liberty and Ellis Island which was her first home when she arrived in the United States. Maryann told me that she was happy to see me and wanted so much to talk to me. We spoke during the whole time of the crossing. She told me that I was like an angel that God sent to her to save her life. She had planned that very day to take her life by jumping off the side of the ferry. She said that she will never forget me because if I had not been there in that critical moment, she would not be having dinner with me now. Naturally, I was deeply moved by her story and later at home I offered a special prayer of thanksgiving to God for having chosen me as His instrument to save a young person's life. Today, Maryann is a very successful health care professional with special empathy for people who like her, suffered childhood trauma.

In July of 1971, my superiors asked me to take on a new assignment. Respecting my vow of obedience, I agreed even though it was not easy to leave Staten Island after fourteen years. I loved the work I was doing: teaching young men preparing for the priesthood as Scalabrinians, doing weekend pastoral work, doing counseling and social work, and teaching religion to adolescents.

It was particularly hard for me to leave my confreres and the friends I made during those years—people such as Sam Panepinto, who was my supporter and right-hand man in youth ministry, and Terry and John Valitutto, who were teenagers at the time but who later married and kept in close contact with me all the years that I was in Canada. In fact, they came to visit me in Vancouver, in Kamloops, and in Chicago after I retired. There were others like the members of the Men's Club, Rose Miranda and the Ladies Auxiliary of St. Charles, and many others, especially the Scalabrinian Sisters who looked after our domestic needs with such care and devotion.

I was hoping that my new assignment would bring me closer to my family in Chicago. It did not work out quite that way. My new assignment would be as pastor of St. Stephen's Church in North Vancouver, British Columbia, Canada. I had been to eastern Canada but never to the west coast. The provincial, Fr. Sordi, had always been very close to our family so I owed him one. In fact, I was honored to preach the homily at the sixtieth anniversary of his ordination to the priesthood on April 24, 2004, in Mt. Carmel Church in Melrose Park.

To make my way to the west, I picked up a drive-away car from a dealer and drove through Yellowstone Park and other famous places. I dropped the car off at a dealer in Everett, Washington. I was picked up by Fr. Sordi, who drove me to Vancouver. On August 13, 1971, he accompanied me to visit the archbishop, James Carney. The archbishop filled me in on the disturbing situation of the parish. He handed me two huge volumes of documentation, which he asked me to read. That was quite a bit of history for a post-Vatican II parish that was only seven years old. I didn't know what I was getting into, but it was too late for me to turn back. I quickly learned that the parish became famous across Canada not so much for the fact that Prime Minister Pierre Trudeau was married there, but for other reasons. I was the fourth pastor in seven years. Does that tell you something?

Because of a disagreement among the parishioners about the direction that this Vatican II church should follow, the parish was literally split in two. One half of the people broke away and formed their own community. This left the remaining folks with a huge debt on the church building. My mission was to try to reunite the two dissenting groups and reduce the debt.

A few weeks after I was there, Cardinal John Wright came to visit Vancouver. Cardinal Wright was the highest ranking American prelate stationed in Rome at the time. Archbishop James Carney must have filled him in on this "famous" parish. When I met Cardinal Wright, he said to me: "Father, win them over with kindness." I tried.

On Sunday, August 15, at all the Masses I introduced myself as the new pastor. No one had ever heard of me, and they wondered what I was all about. Did Archbishop Carney bring me in from Chicago to give the last rites to the parish? In short, it was a cold reception.

First Communion class at St. Stephen's in North Vancouver, 1972.

Gradually I got to know the people and I loved them. They were very cooperative and encouraging to me. My original three-year assignment turned into almost seven years. I can say that those years were some of the happiest of my life. I always wanted to be a missionary and this was truly missionary work of a different kind. Celebrating the sacraments with them was always a great joy.

On the property of the parish we had a walnut tree. One Saturday at harvest time, I decided to pick the walnuts and shuck them. I had no idea at all about walnut stain. Before long my bare hands were black. I tried very hard to remove the stain but to no avail. It was almost time for the 4:30 p.m. anticipated Mass and my hands still looked totally unpresentable. So I bandaged all my fingers to cover those ugly stains. Before Mass, I told the people: "I suppose you are wondering why my fingers are all bandaged. I would like to tell you that they were severely burned when I tried to rescue a child from a burning building. But it was nothing so heroic as that. I was shucking walnuts in the yard and no one told me I had better use gloves."

It was a joy for me to have a children's choir in the parish. There were about twenty-five children who came every week for choir practice. We would sometimes have a children's Mass, but the highlight of the year was the Christmas concert. In our yard we also had a holly tree that bore flaming red berries just around Christmas time. I thought that a small branch of holly berries would look very nice on the children. I thought the idea was so good that I paid very little attention to the branches with their sharp and thorny edges. So during the performance when the children would move, I heard audible sounds of "ouch", "ouch", "ouch". That was the end of live holly branches for Christmas. The artificial ones would do just fine.

One year during one of our Christmas concerns in the parish hall, one of the young girls took sick during the performance and vomited on stage. Her worried mother ran on stage to rescue her daughter. I asked that the curtains be drawn when I saw some youngsters nearby back away, holding their noses. When the stage was cleaned up and the troops were calmed down, the unplanned intermission was over. The curtain reopened and the program continued. After all, the show must go on.

My successor as provincial of the Scalabrinian community was Fr. Angelo Calandra, c.s. He decided to send me a transitional deacon for a six-month pastoral experience prior to his ordination to the priesthood. His name was Dan LaPolla, c.s. He got pastoral experience and more. He also got an unusual lesson in gardening. On our property, in addition to that infamous walnut tree, we also had several rhododendron shrubs with colorful clusters of flowers. Shortly after the new parish hall was completed, I felt that one side of the building was very bare. I thought that we would transplant two of the rhododendrons to the side of the hall to spruce it up a bit. I was told that these shrubs require lots of water and a somewhat shaded area. Water was not a problem. Rain water was abundant in Vancouver. We thought the shade of the building would be just right. But it was the month of August. Dan and I dug and dug around the shrubs but the roots were too deep. So what did we do? We took out our little tractor, bound the shrubs with chains, and literally ripped the roots out of the ground. Jack Toovey, our faithful organist for the 8:30 a.m. Sunday Mass, was a forester by profession. When he saw what we were doing, he was aghast and said that we had just killed those shrubs. I don't know why, but I said to him: "Jack, trust me." We transplanted the shrubs and fertilized them with fish fertilizer. They turned out to be two of the most healthy-looking shrubs on the property.

On the 20th anniversary of my ordination to the priesthood in 1987, Jack and the parishioners planted a dogwood tree next to the hall in appreciation of my unexpected success in husbandry. The dogwood is the floral emblem of British Columbia. I was pleased because I loved the dogwood flower and the legend behind it. Here it is:

At the time of Crucifixion the dogwood had been the size of the oak and other forest trees. So firm and strong was the tree that it was chosen as the timber for the cross. To be used thus for such a cruel purpose greatly distressed the tree, and Jesus, nailed upon it, sensed this. In His gentle pity for all sorrow and suffering Jesus said to the tree: "Because of your regret and pity for My suffering, never again shall the dogwood tree grow large enough to be used as a cross. Henceforth it shall be slender and bent and twisted and its blossoms shall be in the form of a cross—two long and two short petals. And in the center of the outer edge of each petal there will be nail prints, brown with rust and stained with red, and in the center of the flower will be a crown of thorns, and all who see it will remember."

And, by the way, that dogwood tree at St. Stephen's is still flourishing.

When catechism lessons were given at the parish, I enjoyed going to the classes to speak to the children. One day I went to the 7th grade class and asked them what their goal in life was, what were their desires and ambitions, what they would like to be later on in life. One boy answered me and said: "I want to be a millionaire." I was taken aback at such a materialistic ambition. We know that in history, both past and present, some people have become millionaires honestly and others dishonestly. In any case, as we read in the Scriptures, "Love of money is a root of all kinds of evils, and in their eagerness to be rich, some have wandered away from the faith and pierced themselves with many pains." (1 Tim. 6:10) We have numerous cases of this. In 1923 an important meeting was held in the Edgewater Beach Hotel in Chicago. Ten of the world's most successful financiers were present.

They were:

1) The president of the largest independent steel company;
2) The president of the National City Bank;
3) The president of the largest U.S. utility company;
4) The president of the largest U.S. gas company;
5) The greatest wheat speculator;
6) The president of the New York Stock Exchange;
7) A member of the President's Cabinet;
8) The greatest "bear" on Wall Street;
9) The head of the world's greatest monopoly;
10) The President of the Bank of International Settlements.

Here, then, was a gathering of some of the world's most 'money' successful people.

Twenty-five years later, a check was made to see where these men were then (in 1948):

1) Chas. Schwab died bankrupt, living on borrowed money for five years.
2) Unknown
3) Samuel Insull died a fugitive, penniless in a foreign land.
4) Howard Hopson was declared insane.
5) Arthur Cotton died abroad, insolvent.
6) Richard Whitney was just being released from Sing Sing Penitentiary.
7) Albert Fall was pardoned from prison to die at home.
8) Jesse Livermore, of Wall Street, a suicide.
9) Ivan Krueger, a suicide.
10) Unknown

Apparently, eight of the ten men learned the art of making money but did not learn how to live!

An unambiguous statement of Jesus is recorded in all three synoptic Gospels: "It is easier for a camel to go through the eye of a needle than for someone who is rich to enter the kingdom of heaven." (Mt. 19:24; Mk. 10:25; Lk. 18:25)

While I was still at St. Stephen's, my mother came to live with me for two years. She loved the parishioners and they loved her. My mother enjoyed playing bingo. Some of her friends would take her to play bingo regularly in the neighboring churches. One day I asked her if she was not overdoing it by going to bingo so often. She answered: "Renzo, you keep quiet. I'm helping the church." One summer, she took me to Reno, presumably to visit Lake Tahoe but more likely the casino. With her nickels and dimes she would sit at the slot machine for hours. I would seek her out and invite her to take time for lunch but she couldn't be bothered. So one day I asked her: "Ma, you always complained to us about your arthritis; doesn't it bother your arm to keep pulling that lever down so many times?" She answered: "It doesn't bother when I go up and down. Only when I move sideways." (Like when ironing, perhaps?)

I have so many fond memories of Vancouver and my time at St. Stephen's. Vancouver began to grow on me. It is a very beautiful city surrounded by the coastal mountains. On a clear day, sunny day, the view of the city from atop one of those mountains was a sight to behold. Many times I would take the famous cable car to the top of Grouse Mountain, a popular ski area. However, not quite like Whistler with its fine powdery snow.

One summer day, I decided to drive to the top of Mount Seymour to contemplate the beauty of God's creation. As I drove along, I saw several large blackberry bushes with ripe delicious-looking berries. I decided to stop to pick some of them. Before getting out of the car, I saw some movement among the bushes. It was a young black bear who had the same idea I had. When I saw him munching away, I decided to drive on, trying to convince myself that, after all, I really did not have much of a taste for those scrumptious-looking berries.

While in the parish of St. Stephen's, I met so many wonderful people. Here are a few that I remember.

Mr. Doerr was an elderly German man who came to Mass every morning. When he celebrated his ninety-fifth birthday, we decided to have a special party for him. We had an evening Mass at which I tried to use some of the German I was supposed to have learned in Switzerland but it didn't work. Mr. Doerr enjoyed the evening and the affection shown him by the parishioners. He spoke to us in German, which we could not understand, but you could tell that he was very pleased.

We had several homes for seniors in the parish and every first Friday of the month I would visit them to hear confessions, bring them Holy Communion and in some cases, the Sacrament of the Anointing. There was one lady I visited regularly. She was Mrs. Pratt. She was in her upper eighties at the time. Whenever I entered her room, I would find her seated at her table playing solitaire. So one day I said to her: "Mrs. Pratt, every time I come here, I see you playing cards all by yourself. There are so many nice people in this building. Don't you like visiting with them?" She answered: "No, they are so immature." The average age of the residents was probably around seventy-five. Maybe she's right. Maturity doesn't always come with age.

Another person I enjoyed visiting with was Mr. Jack. He was a Native Indian. He was hearing impaired but was able to read lips, so we had no problem communicating. He had been in the residence for several years. The last few times I visited him, I found his health declining. He was sad and depressed. He said to me: "I don't want to stay here anymore. I want to die on my reservation among my people." According to a Native Indian legend, when an Indian felt that his end was near, he would hear an owl call his name. Mr. Jack must have heard the owl. He returned to his reservation and died among his people. He was laid to rest in his ancestral burial grounds.

While Mom was with me for those two years, her very closest friends were Harold and Renée Stark. They treated my mom as their own mother and my mom loved them dearly. They would take her anywhere at any time. I did the funeral of Renée's mom in 1976. Renée was my mom's faithful bingo partner. Whenever either of them would win, they would treat their friends to a snack at the White Spot after the game. Mom was living in Chicago in 1979 when she celebrated her eightieth birthday. Harold and Renée flew to Chicago to take part in the celebration with our family and friends. Harold and Renée came to Kamloops for my installation as bishop and were present at the anticipated Christmas dinner in my house. Harold passed away in 1984 and I went down to Vancouver from Kamloops to celebrate his funeral. Renée and Harold were good friends not only to Mom and me but to all the Sabatinis. Cicero once wrote: "A true friend is more to be esteemed than kinfolk."

For three years I had the pleasure of having an associate pastor. He was the newly-ordained Scalabrinian priest, Fr. Livio Stella, c.s. He was very good to my mother and she liked him. He was one of those culprits who drove her and her friends to those bingo games. Fr. Livio served the Italian-speaking immigrants of North Vancouver and the people appreciated his pastoral ministry. Fr. Livio would one day be elected Provincial of the Chicago Province and later Vicar General of the Scalabrinians in Rome. He came to Valbona for the fiftieth anniversary of my ordination to the priesthood in 2007 and stayed with us for the weekend.

Once you have
turned back,
strengthen your
brothers.

(Lk 22:32)

UNFORTUNATELY, my tenure at St. Stephen's came to an abrupt halt when in January of 1978, I was elected provincial of the Scalabrinian Province of St. John the Baptist. This meant that I had to leave Vancouver and make my way back to headquarters in Chicago. I enjoyed my role as provincial, which was to help strengthen my confreres in their commitment to ministry within the community. I was very proud of the priests and religious of the province. Although my tenure as provincial was of short duration, I was very grateful to my predecessor, Fr. Umberto Rizzi, c.s., for guiding my first steps. He was pleased when I was named a bishop, and came to my first Mass after my consecration.

As provincial, I had occasion to meet Cardinal John Cody about possible changes of the Scalabrinian personnel in the Archdiocese of Chicago. I was a bit apprehensive about this as the local media did not seem very favorable towards him. I must say that he allayed my anxiety immediately. He was extremely cordial and kind. He said to me: "Father, make any changes you wish and I will endorse them."

I had other occasions to meet him and I found him to be equally gracious. On May 13, 1978, I concelebrated Mass with Cardinal Cody in Holy Name Cathedral for the memorial Mass of Aldo Moro, an Italian statesman. On May 21, my mom's parish church of St. Bede's in Ingleside celebrated its fiftieth anniversary of foundation. I was invited to assist Cardinal Cody at the jubilee Mass. Cardinal Cody met my mom and was so appreciative when she invited him to her restaurant for an Italian dinner. One week later, Cardinal Cody presided at the seventy-fifth anniversary Mass of St. Michael's Church on 24th Street and I was asked to give the homily. On July 6, Cardinal Cody invited me to his home and I enjoyed his cordial hospitality. Did he know something I didn't know about what was to happen a few days later? He never said.

One of the stories that circulated about Cardinal Cody was the following. One day he was walking down the street toward home when he was approached by a thief who held out a gun and demanded his wallet. Cardinal Cody got very nervous and said to him: "You can't do this to me. I'm a cardinal. I'm a cardinal." And the thief answered: "I don't care if you're a blue jay. Just hand over your wallet."

On December 19, 1981, I was pleased to be in Holy Name Cathedral in Chicago with many other bishops to celebrate Cardinal Cody's fiftieth anniversary of ordination. In March of the following year, he took seriously ill. Since I was visiting in Chicago at the time I went to see him in his home. He came down from his sickbed and we had a wonderful conversation. One month later he passed away. On April 29 I went to Holy Name Cathedral to concelebrate his funeral Mass. I was pleased to have known such a dedicated churchman who encouraged me in my life as priest and bishop. I could never figure out why he had such a liking for me. I knew he loved Rome and Italians. Could it be because I was the first Italian-American bishop in the United States who was born in Chicago? Who knows? I'll ask him the next time I see him.

Now let's go back to my story. It was in the early morning of July 10, 1978 that I received a phone call from Archbishop James Francis Carney of Vancouver at my provincial office in Chicago. He told me that Pope Paul VI wanted to name me his auxiliary bishop. He begged me to accept. While I was deeply humbled and stunned by the offer, I was somewhat reluctant because I had just left Vancouver six months earlier when I was elected provincial. I began to wonder if this was not another case of *promoveatur ut amoveatur*. A liberal translation is "You promote someone when you want to get rid of him." Some of my religious confreres suggested (facetiously, I hope) that this was applicable in my case. In fact, someone asked me: "Larry, with your record of past performances, how did you ever make it to be a bishop?" I don't know. I guess the vetting process was not very thorough. It happens in politics. It can happen in the Church.

The appointment as bishop caused me some anxiety I remembered the words of St. Paul to Timothy about the office of bishop:

"A bishop must be above reproach, married only once, temperate, sensible, respectable, hospitable, an apt teacher, not a drunkard, not violent but gentle, not quarrelsome, and not a lover of money. He must manage his own household well, keeping his children submissive and respectful in every way—for if someone does not know how to manage his own household, how can he take care of God's church? He must not be a recent convert, or he may be puffed up with conceit and fall into the condemnation of the devil. Moreover, he must be well thought of by outsiders, so that he may not fall into disgrace and the snare of the devil." (I Tim. 3:2-7)

I thought that this was a very lofty job description. The code of canon law spells out the same (C. 378). I wondered if I was qualified to meet that standard.

In any event, in his phone call to me, Archbishop Carney mentioned that the nuncio— the pope's representative in Ottawa— would be expecting my reply in the morning. I was not to speak to anyone about this except my confessor. I did phone the nuncio, Archbishop Carlo Curis. He told me that my file was on Pope Paul VI's desk awaiting my reply before signing the document. Then he added: "Of course, I know you would not like to disappoint the Holy Father." Since he put it that way, who was I to say "no"? The nuncio informed me that the formal announcement was under papal embargo until July 15 when the appointment would be printed in the official Vatican newspaper, *L'Osservatore Romano*. Early on July 15th, I phoned my mother to give her the news. While she was surprised by my appointment, she also had ambivalent feelings. This new appointment meant that I would be leaving Chicago once again to go back to Vancouver. The following day, Sunday, July 16, Feast of Our Lady of Mt. Carmel, I celebrated an outdoor Mass for the parishioners of Mt. Carmel Church in Melrose Park. It was the conclusion of a novena of preparation for the feast which I had preached there. The crowd of over a thousand people applauded the announcement of the new bishop-elect.

A few weeks later, on August 6, the world was saddened by the death of Pope Paul VI. My nomination as bishop was to be one of his last episcopal appointments.

On August 26, the world saluted the election of his successor, Cardinal Albino Luciani, who chose the name John Paul I. From all reports, his election came as a complete surprise. But as they say in Vatican circles: "The cardinals who enter the conclave as heavy favorites to become pope usually come out as cardinals."

My episcopal ordination was set for September 21, the feast of St. Matthew, Apostle and Evangelist. Pope John Paul I was pope but his papacy would last only 33 days. My consecration took place in Holy Rosary Cathedral in Vancouver. My mom and family came for the celebration. The superior general of the Scalabrinians, Fr. Giovanni Simonetto, also came from Rome. Family friend, Fr. Peter Sordi, c.s. now a major superior in Rome, also came to Vancouver and presented me with a beautiful gold pectoral cross on behalf of the

Anointing of forehead during episcopal consecration by Archbishop Carney. At left, Fr. David Monroe who would later succeed me as bishop of Kamloops, and next to him Bishop Fergus O'Grady, O.M.I., co-consecrator.

Communion to Mom and Ralph in Holy Rosary Cathedral during consecration Mass.

community. On the back was a relic of the True Cross. I cherished this gift, but wore it only on very special occasions. My mother gave me the gold bishop's ring that I wear every day. Present were also Archbishop Curis in his capacity as nuncio, about twenty-five bishops and over one hundred priests.

Since a large crowd of people was anticipated, the rector of the cathedral arranged to have a closed circuit TV in the cathedral hall. It was then that Murphy's Law kicked in. The Mass could not begin on time because the closed circuit blew the main fuse: no lights, no sound system and no organ. After about a half hour of frantic maneuvering, the lights came on partially but the organ began to emit strange sounds, and still no microphone. The homilist had to speak at the top of his voice to be heard in that huge, crowded cathedral. At the end of Mass, Archbishop Carney was scheduled to say a few words but because the microphone was not functioning, he decided to postpone his remarks until the reception in the Hotel Vancouver. After the guests arrived at the hotel, believe it or not, the microphone in that hall was also not working. Archbishop Carney abruptly left the reception without saying a word and not in the best of moods.

To complicate matters further, it is customary for the host diocese to pay for the hotel accommodations of all guest bishops. Archbishop Carney had personally made arrangements with the clerk at the desk of the Hotel Vancouver. However, the clerk did not pass on the message. As a result, every bishop had to pay his own accommodation. Again Archbishop Carney was embarrassed, and infuriated with the hotel management. But the story does not end here. The next morning Archbishop Carney went to the hotel to pick up Archbishop

Curis, the nuncio, and drive him to the airport for his return to Ottawa. He parked the car in front of the hotel. When he came out with Archbishop Curis, he discovered that his car had been impounded. He was compelled to take the Archbishop Curis to the airport in a taxi. The next day, Archbishop Carney said to me that he will never again request an auxiliary bishop as long as he lived. He kept his word.

A week after my consecration, I was to accompany Archbishop Carney to Rome for the "ad limina" visit to see the pope, which every diocesan bishop must do every five years. As we were about to leave Ottawa on September 29, we heard of the death of Pope John Paul I.

Before going to Rome for the funeral, I stopped in the town of Valbona to say my first Mass there as bishop. My relatives and the townsfolk received me with the same affection as when I said my first Solemn High Mass there as a priest twenty-one years before. It was

Reception at door of the church in Valbona for first Solemn Mass as bishop.

After the Mass and banquet in "Il Casone" restaurant high up in the mountains with relatives and friends. L-R, front: Aunt Lucia (another of Dad's sisters), Aunt Celeste and daughter-in-law Rosemary; upper far right Uncle Decimo and Don Giannotti, pastor of Valbona.

October 1, the thirtieth anniversary of my father's death. My mom, brothers Ralph and Joe, and cousin Don surprised me by coming for the celebration. It was truly a pleasant surprise because we had time to spend together.

Upon arriving in Rome, I went to the Vatican in the morning of October 4 to pay my respects to the late John Paul I. His funeral was in the afternoon, with numerous cardinals and bishops taking part.

While still in Rome, I was in St. Peter's Square on the afternoon of October 16 when Cardinal Karol Wojtyła was elected Pope and took the name John Paul II. It was an evening to remember. In his first words from the loggia to the thousands of people assembled, the pope apologized for not knowing Italian very well. One Roman man standing next to us shouted out with the spontaneity so characteristic of the Roman people: *Tímparamo noi*. ("We will teach you.")

It was then time to return to Vancouver and get down to business.

My life as auxiliary bishop had its moments. In addition to my work at the chancery, I was also pastor in Holy Cross Church for two years and Holy Name Church for two years. When I was not on the road, I enjoyed celebrating weekend Masses with my parishioners.

May 26, 1979, was one of the most frightening days of my life. Archbishop Carney asked me to conduct two confirmations up the north coast. I left the airport on a small twelve-passenger plane fitted with pontoons for water landing. The pilot also served as baggage handler and mailman. We made an unscheduled landing on the water in the fishing village of Namu to deliver mail. Eventually we landed at our first destination of Ocean Falls and we tied up at the dock.

The town of Ocean Falls is a very interesting story. It was a very small community on the central coast of British Columbia accessible only by boat or sea plane. Formerly, the town was owned by the Crown Zellerback Paper Company. This pulp and paper mill was shut down in 1973. The British Columbia government bought the town and the mill and kept the town in operation until 1980, at which time the government stopped subsidizing the town and the people protested. To put an end to the protests, the government demolished most of the town's buildings and people were forced to relocate. When I went there one year before, in 1979, my confirmation was to be the last one administered in the local church. Ocean Falls was destined to become another ghost town, not unlike the old gold rush town of Barkerville, which is now a tourist attraction.

At Ocean Falls, I was met by a pilot with a float plane who was to fly me in his single engine two-seater to the little town of Bela Coola where I was to confirm some children. It was the trip of my life. It was a cloudy, rainy day. The pilot told me he was from Saskatchewan (probably a crop duster) and was not familiar with the coastal mountains of British Columbia. Not a very encouraging introduction. After we took off, the pilot opened a map which he placed across his lap and consulted it in flight. The noise of the engine was so loud that he gave me ear muffs. Rain found its way into the plane. It was falling on my head from a leak in the roof. He gave me an old magazine to cover my head. I guess he had run out of duct tape. My confidence level was diminishing by the minute as he piloted the plane in and out of the clouds. It was about a half hour ride but it felt more like three hours. As I looked out the window I realized how close we were to the sides of those snow-capped mountains. Finding an opening in the clouds to land the plane in the water was another tense moment. He tried several times to put down but had to pull up abruptly.

Finally we did make it, thanks be to God. By this time I was a basket case. As he was tying up the plane at the dock, he asked me how long the service was going to last. I told him probably about an hour and a half. He then told me that when the service was over I could find him in the pub. In the pub? Believe me, that was to be the fastest confirmation I ever administered. I told the people I could not stay for the reception. I walked to the pub as fast as I could and dragged him out. We then headed for the dock.

When we got there, the pilot looked up at the sky. The clouds were getting darker and darker and the whitecaps in the ocean were getting higher and higher. Then he built up my confidence even more when he said he didn't like the looks of things and that we should get out of there as soon as possible. Did I have a choice? The return trip to Ocean Falls was as scary as the trip out. When we arrived there, I was not in the best emotional shape when I confirmed several children in the parish.

When the day was finally over, I had had enough of air travel. Hence, I decided to take the ferryboat at midnight from Ocean Falls to Vancouver, arriving at 7:30 p.m. This was to be the last ferry service ever from Ocean Falls to Vancouver. It was then that I realized why Archbishop Carney wanted an auxiliary bishop.

Obviously, flying in small aircraft was not my preferred mode of travel. Three of my priests in Kamloops were amateur pilots but only twice did I venture to go up for a trip with one of them. Thankfully, those flights were without incident. I remember one in particular which was quite pleasant. Fr. Jerry Desmond, chancellor of the diocese, was also a pilot of a four-seater. He flew me and our business manager, Gary Cooper, from Kamloops to Pemberton. It was a clear autumn day and the ride was very pleasant. The view of the valley and the mountains was breathtaking. After about an hour's ride we landed at the little airstrip in Pemberton. Monsignor MacIntyre picked us up and drove us to Whistler, where we had an important meeting about the building of the church. After the meeting we were driven back to Pemberton where we boarded the plane for our return trip to Kamloops. All went well—both the trip and the meeting.

Another of the three pilots was Fr. Emil. He had patiently built his own little two-seater. One winter he crashed his plane in a snow-covered mountain. For three weeks, search parties were looking for him by air and by foot but to no avail. Obviously, the falling snow had covered the wreckage and the search would have to be resumed in the spring. In the meantime, plans were being made for his funeral in the cathedral. But guess who showed up? Fr. Emil. He had survived that ordeal by drinking melted snow and eating some candy bars he had taken with him. Naturally he was severely shaken by that tragedy but suffered no serious physical injury. However, this did not deter him from wanting to fly again. When the snows melted, the wreckage of the plane was located. Fr. Emil went up the mountain and brought down all of the pieces to the airport in Kamloops. He reconstructed the whole plane. It was so small, it almost looked like a toy. One day he came to my office and invited me to take a ride with him in his reconstructed plane. I said to him: "Emil, I appreciate your kind invitation but I'm going to take a pass on this one." At least it was more honest than saying that I had an important engagement or some such thing.

There were still other hazards in the life of a missionary bishop. Flying in small planes was not the only one. Driving a car in the mountains in all kinds of weather was no picnic either. I generally drove my own car and I remember three instances that caused me serious trepidation.

At the time of my arrival in Kamloops from Vancouver with my Ford, I knew little or nothing about black ice. Vancouver's roads and highways were generally free of ice—but not rain. One day I was making a turn on a paved road high on a mountain and did not know what to expect around the bend. It was black ice. The car began to skid. I mistakenly put on the brakes and turned the steering wheel in the wrong direction. The car spun around and I found myself on the opposite lane. Thankfully there was no oncoming traffic. I was able to get the car back on course and gradually wended my way downhill in low gear and with many prayers.

In June of 1986, I was to do a confirmation in the small community of Bridge Lake. There were two roads to get there. One was a paved road along the Thompson River and the other was a gravel road over the mountain. The traveling time was about the same but I felt adventurous and decided to take the latter. Big mistake. When I got near the top of the mountain, there was such an intense fog (or better, a low cloud) that I could not see a foot in front of me. I was afraid to stop lest a car or a logging truck would strike me from behind and send me over the ledge hundreds of feet below. I kept going very slowly and as close to the side of the mountain as I could. Again, no oncoming traffic. When I made it down to town I was in a rather nervous state. Naturally, after the confirmation, I took the paved road home.

In March of 1998, another scary moment. By this time I had realized that I should really be driving a four by four. I'm glad I did. The people of the mining town of Logan Lake asked me to do an evening Lenten service in their ecumenical chapel. The town was high up the mountain near the Highland Valley copper mine. Getting there was fine. Coming home was a problem. As I approached the top of the mountain on the Coquahalla Highway, I ran into an ice storm. The road was a sheet of ice. The radio advised all travelers to avoid the highway. I was too far up to turn back. As I inched my way along, I counted twelve cars rolled over in ditches. The police and ambulance crews were passing out blankets. I was able to keep the vehicle steady at five miles an hour and in low gear as I descended the mountain. I finally made it home in three hours for a trip that would normally take forty-five minutes. When I got into the house, the phone was ringing. Several parishioners who were worried were calling to see if I made it home safely. Thanks be to God, I did.

Traveling by small plane or automobile can have its scary moments. But what about traveling by boat? Let me tell you a story. When I arrived in Kamloops as bishop, I learned that each year the diocese rented a small cabin from the Native Indians. It was on the "Little River" which flowed into the huge Shuswap Lake. During the summer, many of the priests would join me for a day of R&R. A few of us pitched in and bought an eleven-foot inboard/outboard boat. There was swimming and water skiing. I was happy to pilot the boat for the skiers. In the evening we would close the day with a nice barbeque. I played chef wearing my favorite apron with the words: "Watch out, McDonald's." During the summer we would keep the boat tied up at the pier on our property. At the end of the season we would take the boat to the marina on the large Shuswap Lake for storage. One year I asked one of our young seminarians to accompany me on this trip. It was a cloudy and rainy day and we had the boat cover on so we would not get wet. The trip down the river was fine but as soon as we entered the huge lake, the wind was blowing and high whitecaps were visible. We had on our life jackets, and I tried to maneuver the boat as closely as I could to the shore just in case we had to swim to shore. At one point a huge gust of wind swept the boat completely out of the water, propeller and all. Thankfully, it landed right side up. It was then that I knew how the apostles felt when Jesus was sleeping on the boat during a storm. We eventually made it to the marina. The employee at the marina looked at us quite quizzically. He was probably thinking: "What are these two crazies doing on the lake in these conditions?" In fact, there was not one single boat on the lake when we arrived there. Enough of that. We eventually sold the boat.

And what about traveling by horseback? That will come later.

After a lengthy illness, in September of 1990, Archbishop Carney of Vancouver passed away. I was in Rome for a meeting at the time. The archbishop had just completed his seventy-fifth birthday—the age of retirement. I received a phone call from the administrator of the archdiocese. He invited me to take part in the funeral on September 27 in Holy Rosary Cathedral and to preach the homily. I accepted because I had served under the archbishop as pastor for almost seven years and as his auxiliary for four years. In the homily I focused on two qualities which to me were very evident in the life of the archbishop: his love and devotion to the Holy Father and his complete adherence to the teachings of the magisterium and directives of the Holy See. This latter sometimes put him at odds with some of the more liberal and radical elements within the Church. He was undaunted. Under opposition he always held his ground.

There is one episode in our relationship that troubled me for years. When I was Archbishop Carney's auxiliary bishop, I did everything I could to please him. When we were together at meetings I would serve him tea, coffee, dessert, take away his dishes and many other menial tasks. After I was assigned to Kamloops and went to the meetings, I felt liberated. One day as I walked by his table carrying my coffee, I thought I said what was intended as a joke but I could tell he was hurt. I said to him: "Your Grace, how does it feel now to get up and get your own coffee?" It was an obvious misspeak on my part. Another case of my mouth not being how it should have been—namely, hermetically sealed. But there were no lingering hard feelings. When he was in the hospital, I drove those 250 miles from Kamloops to Vancouver to visit him when I could. In two successive years at his request I flew to Vancouver during Holy Week to celebrate the Chrism Mass and consecrate the holy oils in the cathedral because the archbishop was too ill to preside. In the end, all was forgiven.

In April of 1979, a year after my consecration, I received a call from the pastor of my mom's parish of St. Bede's. He told me that since my mom never saw me administer confirmation, he invited me to come to Chicago on May 1 to confirm the children of his parish. I was happy to do so. Before beginning my homily, I asked the young people if they were nervous about being confirmed. Many of them nodded yes, not knowing who this bishop was and what embarrassing questions he might ask them. To calm them I said: "You think you're nervous? You see that little lady seated behind you? That's my mother. If I don't do this confirmation to her satisfaction, it will be a long ride home after the service." Happily, Mom gave her stamp of approval.

On October 5 of that same year, I had the privilege of ordaining my first priest. What a joy and privilege! The man's name was Maynard Boomars, a Missionary Oblate of Mary Immaculate. The ordination took place in his home parish of St. Ann's in Abbotsford, British Columbia. Years later, he was assigned to the Diocese of Kamloops and served about twelve Indian reservations with great zeal.

Ordaining my first priest, Fr. Maynard Boomars, O.M.I.

In June of 1981 I was pleased to go to Chicago to concelebrate the 25th anniversary of priesthood of my novitiate classmates.

On March 18, 1982, I celebrated the twenty-fifth anniversary of my ordination to the priesthood. This was while I was pastor of Holy Name Parish on Cambie Street. Archbishop Carney was there,

Celebrating the 25th anniversary of ordination of three of my novitiate classmates: L-R, Fr. Angelo Carbone, c.s., Mrs. Dalpiaz, her son Fr. Alex, c.s., Mrs. Corrao and her son Fr. John, c.s., and my mom.

as well as about one hundred priests and numerous parishioners. Afterwards, an exquisite Italian dinner was provided for all the clergy. Again, it was a day to give thanks to God for the gift of Holy Orders.

To celebrate my anniversary I went to Brazil to visit my relatives, who were anxious to see their nephew or cousin as a bishop. While I was there I went to celebrate Mass in the National Shrine of Nossa Senhora de Aparecida. I noticed the great devotion Brazilians have for their Madonna, not unlike the devotion the Mexicans have for Our Lady of Guadalupe.

My visit to the town of Riberão Pires was very special. This was the town where the Piolis immigrated before the turn of the twentieth century. I remember my Uncle Silvio, who was born there, describing the parish church and surrounding areas. When I went there for the first time, I felt I had already been there—a case of déjà vu?

I celebrated a Solemn Pontifical Mass in that little church. The pastor, a Scalabrinian priest, was extremely welcoming and gave the homily. He got very emotional when he mentioned that a bishop, the grandson of Giovanni Pioli, came to celebrate Mass in this small church to which his grandparents were so devoted. He mentioned that my grandfather's name was on a plaque in the church, a memento of my grandparents' contribution to the enlargement of the church. The parishioners were in tears when they greeted me after Mass. And so was I.

Feed my lambs…
feed my sheep.

(Jn 21:16-17)

ON September 27, 1982, I received a phone call from the secretary of the nunciature in Ottawa telling me that the Holy Father decided to appoint me to the vacant see of Kamloops in the interior of British Columbia. His final words were: "and of course you have no objection". The Holy See seems to have an unusual way of eliciting positive responses. But at least this time he didn't say "the Holy Father has your file on his desk and awaits your answer before signing." The official announcement came on October 1, the anniversary of my father's death.

However, this nomination again caused me some degree of anxiety. The transition from auxiliary bishop to diocesan bishop is an awesome step. A diocesan bishop or archbishop is the head of a special portion of God's flock. He is also called a local ordinary. For example, in Canada there are seventy archdioceses and dioceses. The dogmatic Constitution on the Church of the Second Vatican Council states very clearly that the pastoral charge of the diocesan bishop is entrusted to him fully. He is not regarded as a vicar of the Roman pontiff. He exercises his power in his own right. He is a vicar and legate of Christ. In the truest sense he is termed a prelate of the people he governs. (loc. cit. no. 27)

This sounds like a huge responsibility and I had to think about it long and hard before saying "yes". I remembered the words of Bishop St. Augustine in one of his five hundred sermons:

"The day I became a bishop, a burden was laid on my shoulders for which it will be no easy task to render an account. The honors I receive are for me an ever present cause of uneasiness. Indeed, it terrifies me to think that I could take more pleasure in the honor attached to my office, which is where its danger lies, than in your salvation, which ought to be its fruit. This is why being set above you fills me with alarm, whereas being with you gives me comfort. Danger lies in the first; salvation in the second." (Sermon 340; Pl., 38, 1483)

Additionally, with all due respect, I wondered what the Holy Father had in mind when he named me to Kamloops, a missionary diocese with about thirty-five Native Indian reservations scattered in a territory larger than the whole state of Illinois. Kamloops itself was a town of about 80,000 people. All my life I had lived in large cities: Chicago, New York, Vancouver. I thought I would get cabin fever. As a boy growing up in Chicago I don't remember ever seeing a live Indian. I saw wooden statues of them standing outside cigar stores in some small country towns. I had seen Indians in cowboy movies. They had painted faces, wore feathers and carried bows and arrows. They were generally the "bad" guys going around scalping people. I wasn't afraid of being scalped because I had very little hair to begin with. In my dealings with them, I quickly learned that what was portrayed on the screen was an unfortunate caricature of these fine human beings.

My first contact with Native Indians (or First Nations People) had taken place in October of 1979 while I was auxiliary bishop of Vancouver.

I was invited to say Mass in the very old St. Paul's Church on the Burrand Indian Reservation. The purpose of the visit was to launch a campaign to raise funds to restore the church, which was in disarray. After the service the Indians prepared a barbecue of fresh salmon for all who attended. I was fascinated to see the unique method they had to barbecue the fish. It was absolutely delicious. The event was a typical Indian potlatch. On December 6 of the same year I went to visit St. Mary's Indian School in Mission, British Columbia. It was the feast of St. Nicholas and the Indian youth dramatized the saint's story. After visiting with them and playing floor hockey with them in the gym, I took the opportunity to visit the ailing Chief Dan George, a renowned Indian personality. He was the author of several books: *My Heart Soars*, *My Spirit Soars*, *You Call Me Chief*. At the age of seventy-one he starred in a Hollywood movie with Dustin Hoffman called *Little Big Man*. For his performance he was nominated for an Academy Award for Best Supporting Actor.

In my visit I was able to see the great faith of this man. The walls of his home were decorated not only with many Indian paintings and artifacts but also religious symbols such as the Crucifix, a picture of the Blessed Virgin and the Rosary. Two years later Chief Dan George passed away. The Archbishop of Vancouver was out of town at the time so I was invited to preside at his funeral in Holy Rosary Cathedral. The church was filled to capacity, mostly with Indians from different reservations throughout British Columbia. There were also government officials and some actors from Hollywood. All were impressed with the eulogy of the chief's son Leonard. He described his father as a true lover of his Native Indian heritage and a good Christian-living person.

One of the reasons I accepted Pope John Paul II's request to go to Kamloops was an episode I remembered reading in the life of my model,

Blessed John Baptist Scalabrini. In 1904, just one year before his death, Bishop Scalabrini went to Brazil to meet with his missionaries. While visiting the State of Paranà, he became aware of the many Indians who resided in the interior of the state. These were descendents of those to whom the Jesuits brought the faith a few generations before. Bishop Scalabrini expressed the desire to visit them. As he arrived on the reservation, he was greeted by the Indian chief, who gave him a gift of two cruets that were used in the celebration of Mass. They had belonged to the first Jesuit missionaries who were later exiled by the government. The chief pleaded with the bishop to send them a missionary who could look after their spiritual needs. The bishop was so profoundly moved that he wanted to do something for them. He obtained from the bishop of Curitiba a large parish in which more than three thousand Indians resided. Bishop Scalabrini sent two of his first missionaries to live and work among them. If Bishop Scalabrini could show that kind of love for the Indians, so could I.

After my nomination I chose the date of November 30 for my installation. It is the feast of St. Andrew the Apostle. I had chosen September 21, the feast of St. Matthew, as the date of my episcopal ordination, so now I chose the feast of another apostle for my installation as fourth diocesan bishop of Kamloops. This was a reminder to me that a bishop is a successor of the apostles and I should model my life after theirs.

I was soon to learn that Kamloops had a long history. It was exclusively inhabited by the Shuswap Nation until the arrival of the European settlers in 1811. The word "Kamloops" is a Shuswap word meaning "the meeting of the waters", namely, the North and South Thompson Rivers. The Indians built their encampment at the convergence of these two rivers into the Thompson River. The Thompson merges with the mighty Fraser River, which eventually flows into the Pacific Ocean. What was then a settlement of Indians was to become a city of about eighty thousand people.

Just a few days before the installation, I thought that Murphy's Law was about to kick in again. The airport in Kamloops was fogged in for two days. Consequently, several Canadian bishops could not land. Some of my family and priest friends from Chicago could not make it either. After several unsuccessful attempts to land, they were forced to return to their original place of departure. But at least Pope John Paul II's representative from Ottawa was there to read the official papal document of my appointment. My mom, sister Jenny and her husband Bruno, and cousin Don were present because they arrived before the fog came in.

After I drove Mom from Vancouver to Kamloops, I took her to see the Cathedral of the Sacred Heart. As she walked inside, she had a big smile on her face. She saw a statue of St. Anthony to whom she was particularly devoted. She said to me: "Renzo, I know you will be happy here because you have St. Anthony to protect you."

My installation took place on November 30. Some of my family and friends could not make it. Because of the anticipated large crowd, the installation was held in the Memorial Coliseum, the local hockey arena. About 2,300 people were present including the apostolic nuncio, 25 bishops and about 100 priests (photograph, p. 154). My mother was not feeling well but she endured the almost three hour ceremony. Towards the end of the ceremony, I don't know what came over me. Seeing my mom in such fragile health, I decided spontaneously to speak to her in Italian before that huge crowd. I thanked her for her witness of faith, her love and respect for the Church and priests in particular. I reminded her that my official nomination to the Diocese of Kamloops was on the eve of the thirty-fourth anniversary of my father's death and how he would have been happy to attend the celebration tonight. But he is in a better place. I thanked mom for having lived her many years of widowhood in such exemplary fashion. While I was speaking I could see tears streaming down her cheeks as my voice faltered on occasion. Italians came by bus from Vancouver and understood every word I said. At the end they applauded and cried out "Bravo! Bravo!" I was deeply moved by such a spontaneous reaction. That little speech to mom was so meaningful to me. It would be the last time that I spoke to mom in such a loving and intimate way.

Receiving the gifts at Mass from my ailing mother with Jenny and husband Bruno on her right and cousin Don on her left.

At the end of the ceremony, a group of First Nations People came with their drums to sing the "honor song" to their new religious chief. I was moved by their tribute as they had come long distances to be there. I was very eager to learn more about this portion of my people.

The next afternoon as we were celebrating an anticipated family Christmas dinner in my house, my mother fell seriously ill. I held her in my arms and anointed her. Together with the family and close friends, we recited the prayers of the dying. She was then taken by ambulance to the hospital in an unconscious state. My sister Jenny and I stayed at her bedside. We spoke to her in Italian telling her how much we loved her, hoping that she could hear us. She died the following morning, December 2. I celebrated her funeral in the cathedral that she loved. Ma's body was flown to Chicago for another funeral Mass in the third church of Santa Maria Addolorata. Harold and Renée Stark came to Chicago for the funeral. Her body rests in the Queen of Heaven Mausoleum in the Chapel of St. John Bosco, patron of Brazil. I believe that Ma died from overjoy at seeing how warmly the people of Kamloops welcomed her son, their new shepherd.

Later I wrote the following letter to some of the clergy who attended my installation:

> December 15, 1982
> Dear Friends:
>
> Almighty God in His providential designs has ways of alternating days of joy and sorrow in the lives of His loving creatures.
>
> Last November 30 was for me a day of great joy as I was installed as fourth bishop of the Kamloops Diocese in the presence of my dear Mother and family, numerous bishops, priests, religious and lay people. It was a truly memorable diocesan family celebration as more than two thousand people from near and far gathered to welcome their new shepherd.
>
> On the following day sorrow touched my life as my dear Mother took seriously ill in my home—obviously overwhelmed by the joy and enthusiasm of the day before. God granted me the grace to be with her to anoint her and recite the prayers for the dying, albeit in a faltering way. She went back home to God very peacefully and serenely in the arms of her son—priest and bishop. Mother must have prayed for this grace throughout her life. She always manifested a sincere devotion towards priests as privileged ministers of the Holy Eucharist she so dearly loved.
>
> Please accept my sincere thanks for your kind greetings on the occasion of my installation as Bishop of Kamloops and for the prayers and words of sympathy, extended to me when Mother was called to the bosom of the Father.
>
> As a new year opens up before us, it is my fervent prayer that Jesus the Lord and His holy Mother Mary will smile upon you and fill your days with peace.
>
> Sincerely yours in Christ,
> (signed) † L. Sabatini, c.s.
> Bishop of Kamloops

That they
may become
completely one.

(Jn 17:23)

A diocesan bishop cannot minister to his people all by himself. He needs the help and support of dedicated priests, religious women and men and committed lay people—all working in unison to build up God's kingdom on earth.

When I arrived on the scene in the diocese of Kamloops, there were about forty thousand Catholics and twenty-three priests. About one-third of these priests were Missionary Oblates of Mary Immaculate. These twenty-three priests were responsible for twenty established parishes and about fifty missions, about thirty-five of which were on Native Indian reservations.

The Oblates looked after the majority of the Native missions. The other priests quite often had two parishes to attend to as well as a mission or two. Their weekends were spent traveling from one church to another in this vast territory. I grew to love and admire these priests for their dedication to their ministry.

The diocese was also served by one permanent deacon who was a Native. At one time he was chief of his reservation of Bridge River. Deacon Leonard Sampson and his wife Marie were very active in providing para-liturgical services and religious instructions on several reservations.

The diocese was also served by a few members of the Congregation of Christian Brothers founded by St. Edmund Rice. The Christian Brothers administered and taught at St. Ann's Academy in Kamloops—the only school in the diocese that served students from kindergarten to Grade 12. It was always a pleasure for me every year to celebrate the Grade 12 graduation Mass and attend the commencement exercises. Because of the dedication of the Christian Brothers and their staff, St. Ann's had a reputation for quality education throughout the city of Kamloops. Some of the Christian Brothers were Americans, so almost every year I was invited to their home to celebrate American Thanksgiving with the traditional turkey and the stuffing and all the trimmings.

The diocese was blessed to have religious sisters from different communities serving in various capacities. My executive secretary for fourteen years and at one time Chancellor of the Diocese was Sr. Marie MacDonald, a Sister of St. Martha. The Sisters of St. Martha administered and taught in Our Lady of Perpetual Help elementary school in North Kamloops for many years. The head of our Tribunal and Marriage Office was Sr. Margaret Ryan, a Notre Dame Sister. Her community also taught for many years in the parochial school of St. Ann's in Quesnel in the northernmost part of the diocese. We had Sisters heading the Diocesan Office of Religious Education and the Archives and doing pastoral work in parishes. The Missionary Sisters of Christ the King taught in the Indian Day School in the Chilcotin reservation in Anaham for many years.

Despite all these sisters, I thought there was still room for more. The Daughters of St. Mary of Providence (DSMP) accepted my invitation to come to the diocese. They served in various parish communities.

One of my hopes was to have a contemplative community of Sisters in the diocese. The Discalced Carmelite Sisters from St. Agatha in Ontario accepted my invitation to open a foundation in the west. In April of 1997, the mother abbess, Sister Mary Claire, and two other sisters came to Kamloops from Ontario. Together we searched several potential locations for a monastery. Eventually they settled on a twenty-two-acre farm in Armstrong, the agricultural region of the diocese. Renovations, including the construction of a small chapel, were made to the large farm house to accommodate the sisters. On August 16 of the same year, I officially welcomed the first group of Carmelites to the diocese with a Mass in the chapel of the Monastery of St. Joseph, as it is called. I was so pleased to have the sisters with us. I had always been a devotee of St. Thérèse of Lisieux, the Little Flower, and have worn the scapular medal every day since my youth. It was a joy for me to celebrate with them the feast of Our Lady of Mt. Carmel each year on July 16. It was a day of joy for all the friends of the sisters from the surrounding communities. The chapel was small, so the sisters provided a huge tent on the grounds next to the chapel so that the overflow crowd could assist at the Mass on closed-circuit TV and receive Communion. A luncheon for all participants followed but by rule the sisters were not permitted to join the crowd. As bishop I had free access to their cloister so I would meet with them in the garden and talk about many things, spiritual and otherwise. However, it was not quite like the conversations of St. Benedict and his sister St. Scholastica. They had no popcorn in those days!

The Discalced Carmelites supported themselves by baking the hosts needed for Mass in the parishes. They had beehives and sold the honey. They grew several kinds of fruit and made preserves. They also looked after llamas and alpacas for some farmers. Some wonderful people would bring their farm produce and drop it at the door of the monastery. The sisters had generous benefactors. Armstrong had a widely known cheese factory. Since the sisters are vegetarians, on my visits to them I would stop by the factory and purchase large chunks of cheese to bring to them.

Women of all ages were discerning whether God might be calling them to the contemplative life. The monastery was too small to accommodate them. Before I left Kamloops, plans were in progress for an entirely new monastery which is now almost completed. I can only say that their presence in the diocese was a great blessing. Their daily prayers and sacrifices and spiritual guidance helped to increase the faith life of both priests and people.

Preserve
your traditions
as aboriginal
peoples.

(Pope John Paul II)

ON September 18, 1984, in his pastoral visit to Canada, Pope John Paul II had planned to meet with the First Nations People in the Northwest Territories. However, his plane was not able to land because of the dense fog. He read his message to them from the airport of Yellow Knife.

In his address Pope John Paul II lauded the gratitude that the Indians and Inuit peoples had for the missionaries who dedicated their lives to bringing the gospel message to them. These missionaries shared in the Indians' social and cultural life with respect for their patrimony, languages and customs. The gospel that the missionaries preached to them served to solidify them and ennoble them even more.

The Holy Father told them that while he could not be with them because of the weather, he promised to return to see them at another time. He kept his promise three years later on September 20, 1987. On that occasion, he again praised them for having lived for generations in a relationship of trust with the Creator, seeing the beauty and richness of the land which, as good stewards, they tried to conserve wisely. He recognized and encouraged their efforts to consolidate their traditions and rights as Aboriginal Peoples.

The First Nations People residing in the diocese belonged to five different tribes: Shuswap, Chilcotin, Lil'wat, Okanagan and North Thompson. The largest group was the Shuswap, with nineteen reservations in various areas around the Shuswap River and Lake.

One of my early visits as bishop was to the Indian Reservation of Mt. Currie, the largest in the diocese, numbering about one thousand people. I celebrated Mass in their church (photograph, p. 154) dedicated to St. Christopher and baptized an infant. After the final blessing, the Indian chief approached the altar carrying a bundle of sticks. He asked me if I knew what they were. I thought that they resembled what my father would brandish in his hand to prevent any possible misbehavior on my part but I was not about to tell that to the chief. He said to me that the sticks were called "discipline sticks". Just what I thought. But he was quick to tell me that the stick was not meant to discipline the body but rather the mind. He told me that as a young boy, whenever he had a problem he would go to his father for advice. His father would give him the "discipline stick" and tell him to take it alone into the wilderness. Holding the stick in his hand, he was to pray to the Great Spirit for enlightenment. He told me that as chief he was empowered to give me a stick and that I was authorized to give it to someone provided he/she would respect the Indian tradition of the stick.

When I was back in Kamloops, I visited the parochial school across from the Chancery Office and showed the children the discipline stick. I told them the Native Indian story behind it. Immediately one of the hands in the room went up. One of the boys wanted to borrow the stick, so I gave it to him. He then went to the remotest area of the playground with stick in hand to pray to the "Great Spirit", or the Holy Spirit in our terminology.

Almost every year I would celebrate Mother's Day on the Okanagan Reservation. We would have first communion, confirmation, an outdoor procession with the recitation of the rosary and the crowning of the statue of the Blessed Mother. The Okanagans loved the rosary. Whenever I visited them, I went supplied with a box of rosaries made by our people in Kamloops. I gave one to all the mothers together with a fresh rose.

Very often when I went to celebrate Mass in a church on a reservation, I would find a number of large buckets of water around the altar. The Indians wanted me to bless the water, which they would take home after Mass. They would bless themselves in the home and parents would bless their children with it.

Every year on December 12, the feast of Our Lady of Guadalupe, I would go to celebrate this feast on one of the two Okanagan reservations. The Indians had a strong devotion to Our Lady of Guadalupe because she appeared to an Aztec Indian, San Juan Diego. After the Mass we would assemble in the hall for a party, sometimes featuring a "piñata" for the children.

Every year in August around the time of the feast of the Assumption of the Blessed Virgin Mary, the Indians of Fountain Lake would hold a weekend retreat on the grounds of their reservation. Many Indians would come from afar and pitch their tents near a lake. Instead of a tent, I was offered the luxury of a small R.V. with no water or electricity. Washing in the lake was not my preferred form of bathing. The water was cold, and I was never the adventurous type to begin with. As a city boy, it was hard getting used to.

Quite often I would go to celebrate the feast of Blessed Kateri Tekakwitha on one of the reservations. Blessed Kateri was converted by the early Jesuit missionaries and suffered for her faith. She was beatified by Pope John Paul II in 1982. In many of the mission churches you could see a picture of Blessed Kateri. It was a beautiful sight when teenage girls came to receive confirmation dressed like Blessed Kateri with buckskin dress, long braided hair, a colorful beaded headband and moccasins. Many would take the name of Kateri as their confirmation name. They were so proud of one of their own.

Not long after arriving in Kamloops, I learned from the Indians the difference between clock time and Indian time. One summer I went to administer confirmation to the children of the Chu Chua Reservation outside the town of Barriere. The confirmation was scheduled for 2:00 p.m. I arrived there a little early and there was not a soul in sight. The church was locked and I began to think that maybe I had the wrong date. Nevertheless, I decided to hang around. About 3:00 p.m., I saw a pickup truck come rumbling along the dirt road with a group of young people in the back. As they rode by, they waved to me and said: "Bishop, we are just getting home from a baseball tournament. We're going home to clean up and we will be in church for the confirmation." I didn't mind. If Indian time was good enough for them, it was good enough for me.

The Chu Chua reservation was a very interesting place (photograph, p. 154). The Natives worked well together for the betterment of the community. They cultivated berries and sold them. They built a beautiful assembly area with rooms for their elders, and I was pleased to bless the new facility. I was also happy to be with them to celebrate the seventy-fifth anniversary of their little white church of St. John the Baptist.

Generally after a religious church service we would assemble for lunch or refreshments in the hall. Among some Native tribes it was called the "longhouse". There I noticed something unusual. The elders of the community would be seated all around the perimeter of the hall. Before anyone would touch the food, the teenagers would go to the table and prepare plates of food and take it to the elders. When all of the elders were served, the others would go to the table to help themselves. I noticed that this was the procedure that was followed on all of the reservations I visited. The young people had an enormous respect for the elders. They looked upon them as a source of wisdom that comes from the experience of life. Sometimes after Mass I would set a chair in front of the altar. I would invite one of the elders, who usually occupied reserved seats, to speak to the congregation. When the elder would speak, you could hear a pin drop. The young people especially were wide-eyed as they listened.

The church in Chu Chua, like so many others, did not have running water, so I would have to take water, along with the wine and host, with me from Kamloops for the Mass. I felt we should do something about that. Having to go to the outhouse didn't cut it. I thought that we could build a washroom with running water next to the sacristy. We had very little money so I wrote to the Canadian Church Extension Society for a grant in the amount of $4,000. This was the estimated cost of construction. They sent the money and with the help of the Indians we were able to complete the project. From that day forward, the Indians referred to the addition as "Bishop Sabatini's Washroom".

Native Indians seem to have keen senses of sight and hearing. One day I was visiting a Native family near the beautiful Seton Lake. Across the lake was a mountain with dense trees. At one point, one of the Natives pointed to the mountain on the other side and asked me if I could see the mountain goats. My long-distance vision was very good at the time but I saw nothing. Again and again he pointed me in the direction and still I saw no mountain goats. A little annoyed, he went into the house and came out with a telescope. He pointed it in a certain direction and then he told me: "Now look." I did and, lo and behold, there they were—a white mountain goat and her little one grazing on the steep slope of the mountain. It was so steep I wondered why they didn't fall. Without the telescope I still tried to see them but could not.

In the spring of 1985, I got a very beautiful lesson in Indian life. I went to visit the reservation of Douglas Lake. The Indians were in the process of tanning hides of bucks and moose. It must be said that the Indians have an extraordinary respect for life. They do not hunt or fish for sport but for food which they share with the community. They skin the hides and tan them. When I visited them, they took me to the tanning house. There I saw several Indians, both men and woman, seated along the wall of this smokehouse. One had a long pole with a sharp spear and would scrape the hide until he/she was tired. Then he/she would pass the spear to the next one in line. I decided to join the group and took my turn at scraping the hide. When the skin was supple, they would use it to make such things as clothing or vestments for use in their church. I definitely don't recommend using those vestments in the summer. They are very heavy. They also made moccasins and gloves. They would also paint the skins with images such as the fourteen Stations of the Cross for use in church. What a great lesson for a city boy!

I received from them several pairs of gloves and moccasins and even a necklace with my coat of arms on it. This was beaded by two Shuswap women from the Dog Creek Reservation, who worked two years to complete it. I wore it with great pride and joy whenever I visited any of the reservations and explained to them the profound message they wished to convey. It was all about the church, the Christian community, the bishop, the Eucharist and the figure of an Indian Christ who shed His blood on the cross to save all the races of mankind.

When I made my first visit to the Anaham reservation in Chilcotin country, the Sisters of Christ the King invited me to visit the local Indian school where in addition to teaching religion (since all the children were Catholic), they also taught other subjects such as home economics. The high school teenagers were excited about the visit of their new bishop. They knew that I was an Italian from Chicago. They thought that for lunch they would surprise me by making pizza—Chilcotin style. We all sat and enjoyed it but it was definitely not a Chicago pizza.

On another occasion, I visited the Stone Reservation in Chilcotin country (photograph, p. 153). I said Mass for the people. Before Mass in their Church of St. John the Baptist, some of the elders wanted to go to confession. They knew no English and I knew no Chilcotin. We got along famously. They confessed in Chilcotin and I absolved them in English. After all, God reads the secrets of the heart.

After Mass that day, a middle-aged woman who knew both English and Chilcotin told me that there were two homebound elders who would welcome a visit from the bishop. I agreed. As the woman entered the house of one of the elders to announce my arrival, the conversation between the two became somewhat heated. After a while things calmed down. I was ushered into the room. The sick woman, with rosary beads in her hand, greeted me with a smile. I gave her a medal of the Blessed Mother blessed by the Holy Father, which she kissed devoutly. When we left the house, I asked the woman what they seemed to be arguing about. She told me that the elder misunderstood who I was. She thought I was some minister who would try to convert her and she got very upset. Eventually she understood and was pleased with my visit, as was the other bedridden elder in another home. You just don't mess with the elders' religion.

Some of the chiefs and their counselors were troubled about the high rates of drug and alcohol addiction on their reservations. Substance abuse contributed greatly to adolescent suicide rates and to deaths in auto accidents. Some of the reservations made concerted efforts to remedy the situation. The chief of the Alkali Indian Band (the Indians call their tribal communities "bands") told me that after many determined efforts, his band was almost 95 percent alcohol free.

One day I visited their reservation for a special tribal celebration. I celebrated Mass in Indian style dressed in my buckskin vestments, gloves, beaded necklace, eagle feather and moccasins. In our liturgy, we are accustomed to an entrance hymn as the celebrant enters the church. Not so for the Indians. Their procession is sometimes led by a woman elder clad in traditional Indian dress. She carries a plate with burning sweet grass. The smoke from the sweet grass was meant to encourage positive influences and carry prayers up to the Creator, similar to our incense. With an eagle feather the elder would process into church and waft the smoke towards the congregation. She then did the same to the priest and ministers at the altar. All would then direct the smoke over their entire body. This was somewhat the equivalent of our rite of purification.

Following the elder in procession was another elder beating a drum in slow rhythmic fashion. The drum was a special instrument for the Indians of the west, as the peace pipe was for eastern Indians. The drumbeat symbolized the heartbeat of a mother holding her child at her breast. The child recognized the mother's heartbeat and would feel safe and loved. It was easy for them to understand how the Blessed Virgin Mary is the mother of us all and loves us.

After the Mass, we proceeded to the hall where we were entertained by a group of drummers singing their chants. In fact, a few of them had come to my installation ceremony in Kamloops and played the drums and chanted their "honor song" to their new spiritual leader. It was a very thoughtful gesture. Concerned about the sobriety of his band members, the chief of the Alkali reservation told me that one of his best drummers relapsed into alcoholism and was quickly expelled from the group. Despite losing the drummer, his group had won several Indian competitions. Those young drummers taught me how to drum and sing their chants. I had a great time. Dressed as I was with my pontifical robes, they taught me how to dance, which is completely different from our customary style of dancing. The Indians, young and old, line up in a single file forming a circle around the drummers. They move along slowly, rhythmically swaying from side to side and joining in the chants. There is no physical contact of any kind between the dancers. It was an easy dance to learn even for someone like me with two left feet. It was so nice to see how the children and teenagers interacted with the elders, some of whom were well into their eighties. It was just a beautiful family and social event.

Sacraments in renovated Church of St. Joseph on Kamloops Reservation.

One of the oldest churches in British Columbia was St. Joseph's Mission just outside of Kamloops. It was founded in the 1880's. When I arrived in Kamloops, the church was in total disarray. It had not been used as a church for many years. In fact, it was a useful shelter for their animals. I spoke to the chief about this and he was able to secure government funds to repair the church. With the help of a builder and some of the Indians living on the reservation, St. Joseph's was restored to its original state, including the missionary's quarters in the attic. The church had neither water nor electricity, but there was an outhouse nearby. There was great joy in the community when I officially rededicated the church at the Christmas Midnight Mass in 1985. From then on, Mass was celebrated there every Sunday. It has become a truly historical site visited by many. It contains interesting mementos of early missionary days.

In August of 1993, the Canada Summer Games were held in the Hillside Stadium in Kamloops. I attended the opening ceremonies on August 8 and the very colorful closing ceremonies on August 21. As part of the closing ceremonies, a group of Native Indians came with their drums and sang their chants. At a certain point, an eerie silence came over the crowd as two bald eagles appeared soaring high above the sky, obviously attracted by the familiar sound of the Indian drums. It seemed like they felt safe around the Indians. In fact, the Indians always had a deep respect for the eagle because in their tradition it is the bird that flies closest to the Creator. Eagle feathers are held in high regard by them. On occasion they will give an eagle feather to a white man if they consider him a peace-loving friend. I was honored to receive four eagle feathers over the years and I proudly wore them on my mitre whenever I celebrated Mass with the Native people.

Unfortunately, during the year 1991 the relationship between the Native Indians and the Church began to take a downward turn. It was the time when accusations of sexual abuse against some priests at the residential schools began to surface. We had two such schools in the diocese—one outside the city of Kamloops and the other in the Cariboo country. This whole affair became a serious concern for the Church in Canada and for those dioceses with residential schools in their territory.

The Indians were blaming the Canadian government for starting residential schools and the Oblate priests for managing them and abusing some of their children. There were some charges of abuse which were proven. As a diocese, we made several efforts to meet with the various chiefs to discuss reasonable settlements and reconciliation. Early in January, we held a two-day workshop on dialogue with Native Indians. I went to visit personally the Native Indian Senator Len Marchand in his home. As a Church, we were very much in earnest about repairing the serious hurts and reestablishing a good relationship with the Native Peoples. Finally after several attempts, the Cariboo Tribal Council invited me to a meeting to take place on August 14, 1991 in the council office in Williams Lake. It was in this Cariboo area that St. Joseph's Residential School was situated. I took with me my Vicar General, Monsignor MacIntyre, Chancellor Fr. Jerry Desmond, and the local missionary, Fr. John Brioux, O.M.I. We drove the 3½ hours to their office. There we met with four area Indian chiefs and their executive secretary. The reception was anything but cordial, understandably so. They were anguishing because of the hurts of their people. While the Indians' major target was the Canadian government, they also wanted to draw the Church into the mix in terms of compensation. While the government acknowledged that it was the major player in the lawsuit, it, and also the Indians, wanted to involve the Diocese of Kamloops in the negotiations because the offending priests were given faculties in the diocese.

In order to calm this volatile situation, Bishop John Fergus O'Grady of the Diocese of Prince George, myself and a few Oblate priests held an educational and exchange workshop on June 4, 1992, in the Spallumcheen Community Hall of the Upper Nicola Indian Band. Approximately one hundred people came to hear band members speak about their experience in their residential schools. Chief Scotty Holmes greeted us and expressed the hope that this would be one of many such gatherings. For almost three hours about twenty-five members responded. For most, life in the residential school was a mixture of sad and happy memories. In closing, I thanked the chief and all those who shared their experiences at the school. I agreed with Chief Holmes that we should continue these meetings. It was our sincere hope that any wrongdoing of the past never happens again in the future. I suggested that now was the time for inner healing, which can be accomplished by people of good will. The meeting adjourned after many handshakes, hugs and tears.

The conversations continued for several years. In the end, all parties agreed that it would be in the best interest of all if the matter were settled out of court. On September 23, 1998, and again on October 28, we met with our respective lawyers in the Vancouver Court House. With the help of a court-appointed mediator, we did come to an agreement.

Years later the federal government accepted almost full responsibility for what happened in the residential schools. After all, they were not Catholic schools but government schools. The Diocese had no authority over residential schools as it has over Catholic schools of which the bishop is Chairman of the Board.

While all this turmoil was going on, it was important to continue visiting and ministering to the Native Peoples as though nothing were amiss. Several of them had no animosity towards the Church but had great respect for those missionaries who left Europe almost two hundred years before to proclaim the gospel to their ancestors. This same attitude prevailed toward their current missionaries.

On May 9, 1993, I had a memorable visit with the Chilcotin Indians of the reservation in Nemiah Valley with its church of Mt. Carmel just at the end of the beautiful Konni Lake (photograph, p. 155). This was to be a day of great celebration. It was the day of confirmation for several of the children. For the occasion, they wanted me to bless a huge wooden cross that they made for their ancestral burial grounds. This was to replace the cross which was planted there by their first missionary about 150 years before, and was now rotting away. They pitched their tents along the banks of the crystal-clear Chilco River (hence the name Chilcotin). There they awaited the arrival of the bishop and their missionary. It was normally about an eight- or nine-hour drive by car. The Oblate missionary, Fr. John Brioux, suggested that I fly there because the journey by car would be exhausting. He told me that an Oblate missionary would be available to fly me there if I wished. His name was Fr. Brian Ballard. He had already crashed two planes and came out of them unscathed. He earned the title of "Crash Ballard". Obviously I was not too thrilled about the idea. I had not entirely forgotten my adventures with small planes a few years before.

But I placed myself at the mercy of God and took a chance. This meant a three and a half hour trip by car to the airstrip in Williams Lake where his plane was parked. When I got there, Fr. Brian and a photographer were waiting for me. The single-engine plane was a four-seater and the photographer came along to take photos of the historic event of the raising of the cross. With Fr. Brioux, there were four of us on the plane. It was a beautiful, clear day and the one-hour flight did not cause any apprehension. We landed on a short airstrip of a hunting lodge high on a mountain. There, hereditary Chief Charley Boy was to meet us on horseback. He brought with him two horses, one for me and one for Fr. John. He was supposed to have met us at 10:00 a.m. for an 11:00 a.m. confirmation. As we waited, it was cold on that mountain so we huddled alongside the plane to keep warm. About 11:00 a.m. Chief Charley Boy finally arrived with the horses. His excuse for being late: "I slept in." This meant that the whole program for the day had to be revised. Now we would have to eat lunch first, then the confirmation, followed by the raising of the cross. This raising of the cross in the ancestral burial grounds was very important to the Native people (photograph, p. 157).

The whole idea of travelling down the mountain on horseback did not excite me. I never liked horseback riding for some reason. Did I maybe fall off the horse on a merry-go-round as a child? It was a half-hour ride down the mountain towards the Chilco River where the Indians were awaiting our arrival. The road down the mountain was extremely narrow and I prayed that the horse would know where he was going. Throughout the ride, my eyes were riveted toward the side of the mountain and not to what lay below on the other side. When we reached the camp grounds, I was greeted in English by the rather young-looking elected Chief who said to me: "Bishop, do you remember me?" With eight thousand Indians to look after, that was a difficult question. He saved me by saying: "You confirmed me ten years ago. And do you remember what you told me when you confirmed me?" Now I was really in trouble. He added: "You said to me: 'Young man, you are a really fine person and one day you will be the chief of your people.'" With great emotion he said: "You were right. Now I am the chief." I am no prophet by any means, so he was giving me more credit than I deserved. But then I wondered how many other Indians I might have said that to.

Before lunch began, the chief gave his official greeting to me in English and Chilcotin. The lunch was abundant: smoked salmon, moose, salads, bannock (bread) and desserts. Not bad, except that I would have liked a good old American hot dog. But we were in Chilcotin country.

After lunch we prepared for confirmation. It was pretty cold up there. The Indians prepared a bonfire and placed a portable altar next to the fire. The buckskin vestment and the beaded gloves and warm mukluks surely came in handy. The nine or ten candidates were seated around the altar. During the homily, I was surprised to see how attentive they were to what I said, maybe because I was an elder and they had great respect for elders. After confirmation, one middle-aged woman invited me to visit the place where their ancestors would camp for the winter. I could not believe how those people would be able to survive in those primitive conditions in the cold of winter.

In 1845, Fr. John Nobili, a Jesuit missionary, rode to Chilcotin country on horseback to raise the cross. The new fourteen-foot cross was fashioned by the children of the school in Nemiah Valley.

After the raising of the new cross in the presence of a large number of people from all over the Chilcotin, it was time to go back home. Chief Charley Boy came with the horses and our trip down the mountain was not as scary as going up. We boarded the plane and from the air we circled the area to see the new cross. The Indians below were waving goodbye to us. Our plane ride back to Williams Lake was without incident. I stayed overnight in Williams Lake and drove back to Kamloops the following day. Just another episode in the life of a missionary bishop.

There is, however, a sad ending to this story. Fr. Brian Ballard was involved in a third plane crash. This time he and his passenger did not survive. We also lost a few missionary bishops in small plane crashes. The life of a missionary who serves a huge diocese comes with serious risks. It could have been me. R.I.P.

Thanks be to God, the relationship between the Indians and the Church gradually began to improve. On Pentecost Sunday, May 31, 1998, the chief of the Kamloops Indian band invited me to the new pow wow grounds for an outdoor confirmation Mass. It was a beautiful sunny day and I was attired in my complete Indian vestments. I confirmed 160 young people as 1,500 Natives from all the surrounding bands participated in the ceremony. It was the beginning of a new dawn.

On December 6, I was invited to the Shuswap mission of Alkali Lake for Mass and the blessing of the new church of St. Thérèse of the Child Jesus (photograph, p. 156). During the Mass in which several children made their first Holy Communion, I read a formal apology to them as part of the process of reconciliation and healing. I was so grateful to God to see how the warm relationship between the Natives and the Church was coming back to life.

I learned so much about Native Indian culture and traditions. I tried very hard to impress upon them that they were not second-rate citizens of the Church because they lived on reservations. They were equal members of the family of God, created in His image and redeemed by the Blood of Christ.

The Natives gave me many gifts representative of their culture. For example, they gave me a pectoral cross made of moose bones, with a crucifix, a necklace of deer hide with a beaded Indian symbol in the center, and several other mementos that I hold dear.

One day they presented me with a dream catcher. It was an object made out of strands of fiber in a web encircled by a small willow hoop. I had not seen one before and had no clue what it meant. They told me that it was meant as a charm to be hung over a child's bed to protect the child from nightmares. But as the dream catcher was made of willow and fiber, it was not to last forever. It was intended to dry out and collapse when the child entered adulthood. It was an interesting concept and looked nice on my wall. However, I was quite happy with the crucifix over my bed.

Another object they gave me was a medicine wheel. The wheel symbolizes the individual spiritual journey that each person must take to find his or her own path in life. Within the medicine wheel are the four major directions. Everything in the world comes from these four directions. The wheel's circle represents the circle of life. The Great Spirit caused everything in nature to be round: the sun, sky, earth and moon. The four winds travel in that circle. Each of the four directions has a color: white is the south and represents innocence; yellow is the east and represents enlightenment; red is the north and represents wisdom; black is the west and represents power.

On one of my visits to the Indian reservation of Anaham, we did a ceremony of the Blessing of the Four Directions. I was seated on

Blessing of the Four Directions.

a wagon with the chief and some of the elders as we traveled around the reservation, blessing the homes and the band offices.

There were two other Indian practices that I learned about but never took part in. One was the sweat lodge. This heated and smoky tent was where the Indians went to experience a cleansing of both body and soul. The sweat removed the impurities of the body. When the Indian suffers the heat and perspires, the spirit is cleansed and negative thoughts are released. Some Indians made regular use of this ritual.

The other practice is somewhat similar. It is called the smudging ceremony. It is simpler than the sweat lodge and is commonly practiced by oneself. It consists in burning herbs for emotional, psychological and spiritual purification.

As I traveled to and from the many Indian reservations in the more remote areas of the diocese, I saw some interesting sights that I will never forget. One day I was driving home from a weekend Marriage Encounter on a road with a stream of water alongside. As I looked down the road, I saw two animals drinking from the stream. I slowed down, trying to determine what sort of animals they were. They didn't look like horses or cows. And then I realized they were moose—a mother and her little calf. When they spotted my car, they quickly scampered back into the woods. What excitement! I had seen pictures of a moose with its large body and spindly legs, but this was my first look at a live moose and it would not be my last.

Another time I was driving on a dirt road in a very isolated area in Cariboo country. Obviously, very few cars ever traveled that road. Alongside the road there was a pond. On the side of the pond, I spotted a moose. She had apparently gone for a drink and while she was there, she gave birth to her little one. I stopped the car and could not believe my eyes. I was watching the birth of a moose and I was less than fifty yards away. I wish I had had a camera. After giving birth, the mother saw me in the car, and I shall never forget the frightened look in her eyes wondering whether I was going to harm her offspring. Heaven forbid! I saw vultures circling above waiting to feast on the afterbirth. I sat there watching the mother cleanse the newborn with her large tongue. It was not very long before the little one got up on its thin legs and the two of them slowly returned to the wilderness. I sat there speechless, marveling at the wonders of God's creation. This was quite a different scene than what I saw as a boy in the stockyards of Chicago.

Witnessing the birth of new life in the animal kingdom was always a very moving experience for me. In the northwest section of the diocese of Kamloops, there are many cattle ranches. One of them is the Gang Ranch. It was one of the most impressive ranches in North America. At one time it was considered one of the largest and most famous ranches in the world, occupying over four million acres of land with thousands of cattle and horses. There were also several smaller ranches in the area. In my many trips to visit the missions, I would find myself traveling by a ranch during the calfing season, which was around the first two weeks of March. I would park my car near the fence and look out on the range and watch the cows give birth and how they cared for their newborn. Sometimes when a cow was having a difficult time giving birth, the ranchers would be there to pull the calf. The wonders of nature never cease to amaze me. On occasion I was around when the ranchers were branding the cattle. I did not enjoy that as much. Branding was man's creation, not God's.

As a boy I enjoyed cowboy movies. I remember one movie in the 40's with Gene Autry singing: "When it's Roundup Time in Texas". I was intrigued by the idea of a roundup and cattle rustlers, etc. I never thought that I would ever see a live roundup, but I did. One day in the fall when I was driving north on the Cariboo Highway, I saw this thing called a roundup when cattle are moved from one range to another or to market. Several hundred cattle were crossing the highway, and I envisioned some cow ramming my car. I wondered if I would ever get through. The cowhands on their horses did everything they could to create an opening in the road for me to pass. It was not an easy task, but they eventually succeeded and I was able to inch my way through that loud chorus of "moos".

One day as I was on my way to confer confirmation in Cariboo country, I drove through the main street of the town and saw a sign on the local pub. It read "The Branding Iron." I suppose it was a place where the cowhands hung out. As I drove by, an idea flashed across my mind. I thought I could use the analogy of branding when speaking to the confirmands. After all, branding was something these young people were very familiar with. Cattle raising was their family livelihood. They knew that the young calves

Church of St. John the Baptist on Stone Reservation—built in 1904 (same year as Holy Rosary).

Processing into the Memorial Arena for my installation as bishop of Kamloops.

After baptism in St. Christopher Church in Mt. Currie.

Confirmation in Chu Chua Reservation with Sr. Marie Gartner, S.M.S.

Our Lady of Mt. Carmel Church on Nemiah Valley Reservation (Konni Lake on left).

The Journey Team in front of diocesan retreat center.

After dedication of new log church of Bl. Kateri Tekakwitha in Alexandria Reservation on west side of Fraser River, 1984.

Our Lady of the Mountains in Whistler-Blackcomb.

Confirmation in Church of St. Thérèse of the Child Jesus on Alkali Lake Reservation. Top right: Fr. Maynard Boomars, O.M.I.; bottom right: Sr. Evva Melanson.

Groundbreaking for Church of Our Lady of the Valley. Fr. Ray McLeod behind Cross.

New log church of St. Paul on Canoe Creek Reservation, 1986.

After 50th wedding anniversary ceremony of Maria and Eddie Alexander in new Alexandria church.

Raising of the Cross at Big Lake, one of the ancestral village sites of the Chilcotin people, Mother's Day, 1993.

Confirmation during blessing of new log church of St. Augustine in Canim Lake.

Above: After dedicating new log church of Our Lady of Lourdes on Quilchena Reservation.

Below: Baptism in new church in Canoe Creek.

NEXT PAGE
Top: Members of Latino community. To my left, Deacon Jorge Rozo and below him, his wife Nubia.

Bottom: Episcopal Vicar Bishop John Manz at the installation of Fr. Michael Kalck (at right of the bishop)

Above: Dedication of the Shrine of the Immaculate Heart of Mary in Cache Creek (on right, Deacon Leonard Sampson).

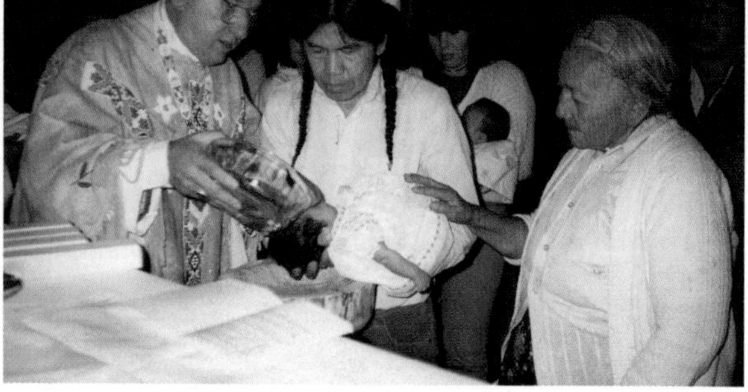

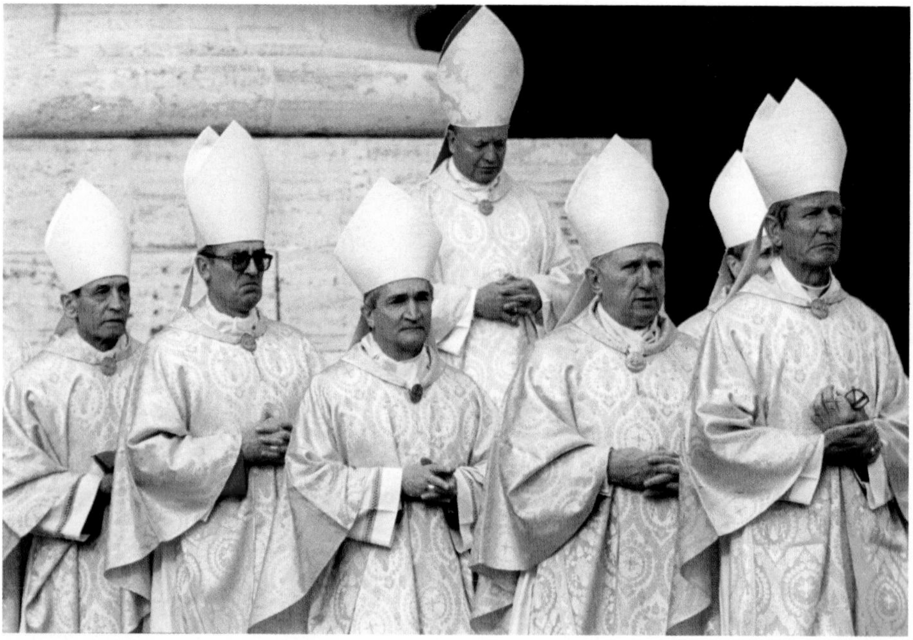

Procession to the outdoor altar in St. Peter's Square for concelebrated Mass with Pope John Paul II for beatification of Bl. John Baptist Scalabrini on November 9, 1997. Scalabrinian bishops: R-L, Bishop Laurindo Guizzardi of Brazil, myself, and Archbishop Silvano Tomasi, Vatican diplomat.

Greeting the Pope after beatification ceremony.

were branded with a red hot iron to signify that those cattle belonged to their family and would be looked after with much care. So, during the ceremony, I told them that confirmation was like a branding. By the laying on of hands and the anointing with the sacred chrism, their souls would be marked with an indelible logo. This meant that they will belong in a special way to the family of Christ. He loves them and will look after them more so then as He does the birds of the air and the lilies of the field. (Mt. 6:26-30) But I told them it is important to stay united to the herd lest they fall prey to rustlers such as the world, the flesh and the devil.

The diocese of Kamloops for seventeen years did have its exhilarating moments for me. For the time I lived there, I was not entirely separated from my religious community. For three years I had in the diocese an elderly but very energetic Scalabrinian, Fr. Gregory Zanoni. He ministered to the Italian immigrants in the city of Kamloops and visited over four hundred families. Due to ill health, he left the diocese and went to the Scalabrinian nursing home near Trento, Italy, close to where he was born and grew up. I visited him there. He died in 1995.

Shortly after the beatification of Blessed John Baptist Scalabrini in 1997, I invited Fr. Gino Dalpiaz, c.s. to join me in a week-long seminar to our Kamloops priests at our Marian Shrine in Cache Creek. The topic of our presentations was: "The Life of Blessed John Baptist Scalabrini and his Relevance in the Life of Priests Today".

I also had visits from several of my confreres: Fr. John Corrao, Fr. Angelo Carbone, Fr. Vince Cutrara. Fr. John witnessed for himself the poverty of the churches in our missions. He talked to several pastors in his New York province and was able to collect and send to me huge boxes of vestments and other church furnishings.

Are any among you sick?…Call for the elders of the Church.

(Jas 5:14)

BISHOPS, like everyone else, are subject to illness, even of a serious variety. It can strike at unexpected times. I had one such close call.

On October 14, 1992, I went to the Shrine of the Immaculate Heart of Mary in Cache Creek to celebrate Mass with children from one of our parochial schools. It was customary for our school children in the diocese to make a pilgrimage to the Shrine during October to honor Our Lady of the Holy Rosary. After lunch with them, I was driving back to Kamloops when I began to feel very ill. I decided to go directly to my doctor's office. He examined me and sent me for an EKG. After viewing it, he sent me immediately to the emergency room of Royal Inland Hospital. From there I was moved to the ICU where I received the Sacrament of the Anointing of the Sick for the first time. My whole body seemed to have collapsed. I was hooked up to an assortment of machines and IV's. That first night was ugly. I woke up in the middle of the night vomiting from the morphine they gave me to ease the pain. As I looked around I saw myself surrounded by a doctor and three nurses who asked me about the intensity of my pain. All I wanted to do was to sleep. Thanks be to God, I survived the night.

The next morning, after I received Holy Communion, my doctor came in. I'll never forget his words to me: "Larry, we haven't yet figured out what is wrong with you, but don't leave us now." I felt very weak but did not think I was that close to checking out.

The next morning one of my young priests brought me communion. He was Fr. Dale. I had ordained him about six months before. I had tears in my eyes when I said to him: "Dale, I don't know if I will ever get out of this bed and celebrate another Mass. But every day you celebrate Mass, say it as though it were to be the last Mass of your life." He nodded assent.

After four days in intensive care, I was moved to a private room in the hospital. I was to spend a week there. Before releasing me, my doctor came to the room and said to me: "Larry, it is stress that has almost killed you. Next time you may not be as lucky. You must go away from Kamloops and spend at least one month in convalescence somewhere." I took his advice and went to the Scalabrinian rest home in Sun Valley, California. There I was still not feeling well and made several trips to see a cardiologist in St. Joseph's Hospital in Burbank. It is known as Bob Hope's Hospital.

After more than a month of convalescence, I returned to Kamloops. I realized that I could no longer burn the candle at both ends. I revised my daily schedule. It took more than a year before I felt I had regained control of my body. The Lord was truly good to me. However, it was kind of humbling for me to notice that even with an absentee bishop and later, one of limited strength, the diocese got along quite well.

My experience in the hospital served to heighten my appreciation of the ministry of visiting the sick and the dying in their homes or in the hospital. It comes with its rewards. "I was sick and you visited me." (Mt. 25:36)

Let the
little children
come to me.

(Mt 19:14)

ABUSE of children is an ugly crime, be it physical, sexual or emotional. When the perpetrator is in a position of trust, the crime is even more despicable. Convicted abusers should be punished to the fullest extent of the law. Jesus loved children, embraced them and He said: "The Kingdom of God belongs to such as these." (Mt. 14:14) Jesus was equally severe in His judgment of those who violated the innocence of children: "It would be better for anyone who leads astray one of these little ones who believe in me to be drowned by a millstone around his neck in the depths of the sea. What terrible things will come on the world through scandal." (Mt. 18:6-7)

A priest is a pastoral minister in a privileged position to work closely with children. As a priest and bishop, one of my pastoral activities was to provide a loving and caring environment within our schools and after-school religious education programs. Aware of the fact that parents are the first teachers of their children, our schoolteachers worked closely with them to provide their children with quality education and sound religious formation.

During my tenure as bishop, we built two new parochial schools in the north of the diocese, one in Quesnel and the other in Williams Lake. We also helped build a one-room schoolhouse in a remote pig farming area called Mabel Lake. The parents home-schooled their children. However, every morning they would bring their children to the schoolhouse where a teacher would go over their work individually. We were very happy to see that the graduates of this school did well when they entered the public high school. I was always happy to go to the schoolhouse to celebrate Mass there. Afterwards we would have lunch with the children and the parents who graciously provided the lunch—pork, of course. It was my custom to visit all the five schools in the diocese on a regular basis.

I enjoyed the fact of having my office in Kamloops very close to Our Lady of Perpetual Help (O.L.P.H.) Church and School. I would visit the classroom often, especially grade three, where I would read to the children the lives of the saints. The children seemed quite interested in the saints as positive role models. The kindergarten class was especially dear to me. I would like to be there for the beginning of the class when the children would offer their spontaneous prayers of petition to God. What they prayed for really came from the heart. They had no inhibitions in expressing their prayerful, intimate feelings.

The kindergarten children of O.L.P.H. were so proud when they were able to sing for me the ABC's. I would try to confuse them by singing them in wrong order. They would stop me and shout: "Bishop, you have them all wrong." And I would ask them: "How can they be wrong? Would my teacher make me graduate if I didn't know the alphabet?" They were not convinced.

The teacher, Sister Lucy MacNeil of the Sisters of St. Martha, had such a motherly way with the children. They loved her and so did their parents. On a few occasions some of the children would come late to school. One day this pretty blond-haired child with blue eyes came to school late with tears in her eyes. Her name was Rachel. She said: "My mother didn't wake me up on time." Sister would seat her between the two of us and we tried to comfort her. Graduation day for these children was always a very special event for the children and their parents. Every year I would arrange my schedule so as not to miss the graduation. I loved to give the children their first diploma. The children looked so beautiful in their paper caps and gowns as they stood on the risers. The parents were moved to tears by the children's warm and loving tribute to them and to Sister Lucy. On the day of Rachel's graduation, toward the end of the program, Rachel announced that they were going to sing the ABC's. Then she pointed her finger toward me and said: "And, Bishop Sabatini, this is your last chance to learn your ABC's."

I went back to Kamloops for the first time after nine years in Chicago. I visited O.L.P.H. School and said Mass for the school children. Lo and behold, there in the back of the church was Rachel with her three small children. After Mass we talked for a while and she recalled her kindergarten graduation with a huge smile on her face. Her oldest child is now in O.L.P.H. School. Rachel said to me: "I just love this school." I always knew that Rachel was a bright girl. She gave me a picture of her holding another diploma much more meaningful than the one I had given her in kindergarten. It was her Master's degree in social work from the Thompson Rivers University in Kamloops. I was so proud of her.

As bishop in Kamloops, often after lunch I would fill my pocket with candy bars and go out on the playground at O.L.P.H. and mingle with the children during recess. Invariably someone would remind me that it was his/her birthday. It was my custom to give them a candy bar for their birthday. But as children sometimes do, they will try to pull a fast one on you if they can get away with it. Just like little Johnny telling me that today was his birthday. I looked at him and said: "Johnny, didn't we celebrate your birthday two weeks ago?" He replied, "Oh, yeah, I forgot" and he sheepishly walked away.

Then there was the little nine-year-old girl named Tracey with her bushy, flaming red hair. She reminded me so much of "Little Orphan Annie", the comic strip I used to read as a boy. When I saw her lining up before school, I would sing to her a few lines of "Tomorrow, Tomorrow" from the Broadway musical *Annie*. She would smile. Many years later she wrote to me and recalled how (badly?) I would sing to her at school.

In the diocese of Kamloops there is a very well-known place called the Adams River. This body of water is a famous spawning ground for Pacific salmon. People from all over British Columbia and other parts of the country would go there in the first weeks of October to witness the spawning. This takes place in a huge way every four years. People who go there are shown a documentary on the life cycle of the salmon. Then people walk along the banks of the river or onto the viewing platform to witness one of nature's extraordinary sights. Thousands of salmon are seen vigorously swimming upstream for miles without consuming anything but their own protein. When they reach the spot where they were born four years ago, they deposit on the river bed thousands of little round pink eggs the size of peas. They then come up to the surface and die. During the night the bears came out to eat the fish. This would be their protein for the long months of hibernation.

In October of 1986, during the big run, I accompanied the children of O.L.P.H. School on a field trip to the spawning grounds. Having been prepared in class, they went to the grounds with notebooks to jot down the important aspects of their visit. The following day I went into a classroom to ask the children about what impressed them the most about their field trip. One boy raised his hand and said: "What impressed me the most was the stink of the dead fish." He was honest but I didn't think that he had the makings of a marine biologist.

On a sadder note, sometimes tragedy strikes when we least expect it. It happened to us in the summer of 1993. A logging company offered us the use of their logging site as a summer camp for the children of the diocese. It was situated in a remote area surrounded by huge trees. We had use of it for two weeks, one week for the younger children and the other for the older ones. A group of parents would be there to cook and act as chaperones. The diocesan youth leader and a number of young volunteers would be there also to organize the group activities: hiking, boating, swimming, campfires, Mass in the tent, etc. One afternoon, one group of children was seated in a circle when a fierce wind came up and a loud crackling sound was heard. A huge tree was uprooted and was beginning to fall. All the children fled for cover except one boy named Ian. He was struck by the tree. He was rushed to the hospital but was dead on arrival. I was informed of the accident and drove frantically to the hospital to see him. When I entered the room, I saw the mother holding her dead eight-year-old child in her arms and singing to him a sweet lullaby as she probably had done many times before. When I saw this scene, I was moved to tears. I thought of Michelangelo's masterpiece "The Pietà" where Mary is holding in her lap the lifeless body of her Son Jesus. I was overcome also by a feeling of guilt. If I had not organized the summer camp, this tragedy would not have happened. But it did. And it happened on my watch.

The vigil service and funeral in the family's parish on July 27 brought out a very large crowd of mourners including Ian's schoolmates. I conducted the funeral with the pastor and other priests. The homily that I delivered was most difficult for me and my words were so inadequate when you think of the enormous suffering of the parents and siblings.

Ian's mother had once told me how happy Ian was to have made his first Holy Communion just a few months before. He liked to go to church and receive Communion and looked forward to serving Mass. His parents were so proud of him. He was deeply religious for his age. Who knows? Could he have been a priest some day? Ian's parents would not have objected.

On the other hand, one day I was saddened when a parent of a boy in one of our parochial schools told me why she would not allow her boy to serve Mass. She said that he might like being around the altar so much that he might think of becoming a priest. She blatantly added: "I don't want him to be a priest. I want grandchildren." She did not understand what a gift of God it would be to have one of her children enter the priesthood or religious life. It seems that some parents feel that they own their children—body and soul. How sad for those who impede their children from possibly answering God's call to ministry.

Remember
the Creator
in the years of
your youth.

(Ecc 12:1)

MINISTRY to young people was always one of my priestly priorities from the time I began to do adolescent and family counseling in New York. My belief was that as young people grow and mature in their faith, they should strive to be positive role models and witnesses to other young people. On this premise, early in 1997, we formed a group of young adults ages 18–23. This group met twice a week in the diocesan office with their advisor. Every Wednesday evening and Sunday afternoon they would spend time together for prayer, song, and study of the Bible and the teachings of the Church. These young men and women bonded together so well. I would join them whenever I could for Mass in the chancery chapel and for Wednesday evening supper. When their period of formation was completed, they went to the cathedral where on December 7, 1997 we held the first official commissioning of the "Journey Team" as they chose to be called (photograph, p. 155).

Several of the young people also took part in an abstinence program called "True Love Waits". It has proven to be a solid preparation for marriage. On the same evening of the commissioning, these young people made their public pledge to be chaste till marriage and were given a "chastity ring". They wore the ring with pride and when asked by some, they were not ashamed to tell them what it meant. A good witness to a world saturated with sexual propaganda. After that evening liturgy in the cathedral, a woman greeted me at the door and said: "This service was so inspiring. I only wish that my teenagers would have been here to witness it."

The Journey Team was now ready to spread the good news. The diocese bought them a large van to travel from parish to parish and mission to mission in the vast diocese. They would conduct evenings of reflection, weekend retreats for families and provide music and singing for all the religious services. The parishes that invited the team would provide room and board for the group. The team particularly enjoyed visiting several of the thirty-five Indian reservations and working with the Native youth. It was a new cultural experience for them.

Before Easter of 1998, the chaplain of the Raleigh Correctional

Center in Kamloops phoned to invite me and the Journey Team to celebrate an afternoon religious service for the inmates on Easter Sunday. The team was very eager to accept but also quite apprehensive since they had never been in a medium security prison. All of us had to undergo a detailed security check which only added to their anxiety. After we arrived on the scene and went through a thorough screening process, the young people prepared the altar for Mass. They were ready with their instruments to provide songs and music. When all was ready, the guards walked the inmates into the chapel dressed as they were in their prison uniforms. They were seated on benches. When it came time for the Sign of Peace, the young people were unsure as to what they should do. I encouraged them to give the sign to the prisoners, which proved to be a deeply moving experience for them.

When we had arrived at the prison, the Team wanted to give a gift of a box of oranges to the prisoners. However, because of security, they were not allowed to do so personally. The warden accepted the gift and said he would see to it that the prisoners received it.

When the Team returned home, they were so moved by what had taken place in that prison on that Easter day. They talked about it for weeks.

A few days later, the chaplain of the prison phoned me to say how much the prisoners enjoyed our visit. They said it was the best service they ever attended and wanted the group to come back again. The words of Jesus echoed in our hearts for a long time: "I was a prisoner and you visited me." (Mt. 25:36)

My house
shall be called
a house of
prayer.

(Mt 21:31)

WHEN the early converts to the faith gathered for prayer and worship, they did so in private homes. In the first three centuries during the time of the persecution of Christians, the Church went underground. The Christians worshipped in places where they would not easily be discovered. When Constantine was the Roman Emperor in the fourth century, he became a patron of the Christian Church and effectively ended the long age of Roman persecution of Christians. To accommodate the rising numbers of the faithful, it became necessary to provide suitable assembly areas where Christians could gather for worship. Thus, the first churches were built in Rome.

Jesus Himself recognized the importance and sacredness of worship space. He frequented the Temple. On one occasion He drove out of the Temple those who were buying and selling. He felt that they were turning the Temple into a den of robbers.

To this day, churches continue to be built in those places where the number of Catholics requires one. The diocese of Kamloops was no exception. There were areas where a new church was needed or an existing one renovated or enlarged. Since the Immaculate Heart of Mary was the principal patroness of the diocese, a shrine in her honor was dedicated on her feast day, June 4, 1988, in Cache Creek, the geographic center of the diocese (photograph, p. 158). Since the year 1988 was declared a Marian Year by Pope John Paul II, this was our diocesan project for the Year of Mary.

Walking distance from the Shrine was a little log house which was called the "Poustinia" (a Russian word meaning "desert"). It was a place where people would go for a day or two for a period of total silence, prayer and penance. It was in a sort of desert area surrounded by very small cactus plants.

The shrine was followed four years later by the building of an adjacent retreat house. Devotion to the Blessed Virgin Mary was widespread in the diocese thanks to the efforts of the previous bishops, missionary priests and religious sisters.

I had the privilege of dedicating some new churches in Mary's honor. One was the church of Our Lady of the Valley (photograph, p. 156). The founding pastor was Fr. Ray McLeod. We both had something in common. We shared the same birth date. Fr. McLeod was a retired priest from Vancouver who came to live in the Kamloops diocese hoping for a peaceful retirement. No such luck. I asked him if he would consider founding a new parish in a fast-growing community. He agreed and built a beautiful church. He loved the community so much that before he passed away, he requested to be buried in the Ukrainian Catholic cemetery very close to the church. I could not attend his funeral but I was able to visit his grave and pray for the repose of the soul of this faithful priest and good friend. I also visited the tomb of Msgr. John MacIntyre, my faithful Vicar General for many years.

Other Marian churches founded during my time were Our Lady of the Lake in Sorrento near to the Shuswap Lake and Our Lady of the Mountains, a log church built in Whistler-Blackcomb, two internationally known skiing areas (photograph, p. 156).

Many of the old wooden board churches built by the early missionaries burned, and the Indians preferred them to be replaced by log churches that seemed more durable. In 1983 we had the blessing of Our Lady of Lourdes log church in the Quilchena Reservation (photograph, p. 158). In 1984 I also blessed the new log church of St. Stephen in the Bridge River reservation. The original church was built in 1912. The new log church of St. Paul in the Canoe Creek reservation was blessed in the fall of 1986 (photographs, pp. 157, 158). This was followed by the blessing of the log church of St. Augustine in the Canim Lake Reservation in 1991 (photograph, p. 157).

On October 7, 1992, a church was officially dedicated in Pemberton and given the name of St. Francis of Assisi. It seemed appropriate to name the church in that lovely Pemberton Valley after the patron of the environment. In 1994 we had the blessing of the new log church on the Alexandria reservation, named in honor of Blessed Kateri Tekakwitha (photograph, p. 155).

We also built a church dedicated to St. John Vianney, secondary patron of the diocese of Kamloops. It was consecrated in October of 1991.

Church buildings satisfy a practical need. However, no matter how beautiful they are, church is more than a building. It is a community of faith where people assemble to grow in their spiritual life and where they are offered the resources to help them do so.

When Jesus said to St. Peter: "You are Peter and upon this rock (Peter) I will build my church", He was not referring to a physical structure. We love our churches, but we love the people who frequent them and call their church a home away from home. I not only loved to bless new churches and to celebrate the anniversaries of old ones, I also loved to celebrate our "living stones," our dedicated Christians who built up strong marriages. It was always a pleasure to conduct marriages and significant wedding anniversaries of our Native People, such as the fiftieth anniversary of Maria and Eddie Alexander in 1994 (photograph, p. 157).

Come away to a
deserted place by
yourselves and
rest a while.

(Mk 6:31)

MOST people recognize that from time to time it is important to get away from one's usual routine and occupation and seek someplace for R&R. Such a respite is good for the soul as well as the body. Some people go far away to find their deserted place, seeking to enrich their spiritual lives. We call those journeys pilgrimages. I enjoyed a few myself.

The Holy Land

On July 14, 1970, in the company of twelve other priests and a biblical scholar, I made my first pilgrimage, which was to the Holy Land. After so many years of studying the Bible, I had longed to visit the places which were sanctified by the presence of Our Lord, the Blessed Mother and the apostles. Our first stop was in Athens, Greece, where early in the morning we went up to the Aeropagus to the place where St. Paul delivered his famous speech to the Athenians. There we read the entire speech from the Acts of the Apostles (17:16ff). In it Paul alludes to an altar dedicated "to an unknown god". Paul then spoke about the resurrection of Jesus the known God. Some of the hearers joined him and became believers.

We later flew to Tel Aviv where we visited Nazareth and said Mass in the chapel of the Annunciation. From there to Mt. Tabor where we said Mass in the Church of the Beatitudes.

On July 16, the feast of Our Lady of Mt. Carmel, we visited Mt. Carmel, near Haifa, where St. Simon Stock, a Carmelite priest, lived for some time. A well-known painting of Our Lady of Mt. Carmel shows the Blessed Virgin giving the Carmelite scapular to St. Simon.

We visited Cana where Jesus preformed His first miracle by changing water into wine. Before visiting these holy places we always read portions of the gospel relating to the places we were to visit. In this way it was truly a spiritual experience with time for prayer and reflection.

We took a boat ride across the Sea of Galilee to the town of Capernaum where Jesus gave His famous teaching in the synagogue on the Holy Eucharist (Jn. 6:50-59). While we were crossing the Sea of Galilee, we read about the apostles' famous fishing trip, how Jesus calmed the storm, and how Jesus walked on the water. We remembered the story of a priest who asked a fisherman for a ride across the sea. Knowing he was an American, the fisherman quoted him an exorbitant fee. Disappointed, the priest was heard to mutter, "No wonder Jesus walked on the water!"

We went to the River Jordan to bathe in the waters where Jesus was baptized by St. John the Baptist.

On July 18 we crossed Samaria, stopping at Jacob's well where we read the account of the Samaritan woman. We visited Emmaus and read the account of the people who met the Risen Lord without knowing who He was.

Finally we made our way down to the old Jerusalem where we took up lodging in the Arab part of the city near the Damascus Gate. The following day we visited the Church of St. Peter in Gallicantus, where supposedly St. Peter heard the cock crow after he had denied Christ three times. We also went to Mt. Zion where we visited the Cenacle. We celebrated Mass in the Basilica of the Dormition, which is the Byzantine name for the Assumption of our Blessed Mother. Devotion to Mary's Assumption was widespread long before it was defined as a dogma of faith by Pope Pius XII in 1950.

We also visited the tomb of David and traveled the road to Jericho and the Dead Sea. We remembered the gospel story of the man who was robbed on the road to Jericho and was helped by the Good Samaritan. The Dead Sea is 1,385 feet below sea level and its shores are the lowest point on the surface of the earth on dry land. The Dead Sea is over a thousand feet deep and is one of the earth's saltiest bodies of water. It has no fish and is rightly called the Dead Sea. It is about forty miles long and four miles wide. We did not venture to swim in that sea of brine.

We visited the Qumran excavations and then to Bethany where Jesus used to visit his friends, Martha, Mary and Lazarus.

My trip to the famous "Wailing Wall" (or Western Wall) was memorable. In my anxiety to get to the wall to pray, I did not realize that the men were separated from the women and I found myself in the women's section. A gentle person tapped me on the shoulder and kindly suggested that I go to the other side. Red-faced, I did and prayed as the Jewish men were doing with their heads moving back and forth towards the wall. I was reminded of that holy man who went directly in front of the wall each morning to pray. One day a reporter went up to him and said: "You come here every day to pray so devoutly. Does

In the Holy Sepulchre in Jerusalem.

God ever answer your prayers?" The man answered sadly: "No, I sometimes feel like I'm banging my head against a wall." Don't we all feel like that at times? But God does answer our prayers in His own way and in His own time. Faith is our greatest asset.

Outdoor Stations of the Cross in streets of Jerusalem.

On July 20 we went to the Mount of Olives and the Garden of Gethsemane where Jesus endured His agony while the apostles slept. We were quite awake as we read the gospel account of the agony. We visited Abraham's tomb in Hebron and from there to Bethlehem where we celebrated Mass in the Grotto of the Nativity.

July 21 was the highlight of our pilgrimage. We celebrated Mass in the Holy Sepulchre at 5:30 a.m. We also made the outdoor Stations of the Cross retracing the steps of Jesus on His way to Calvary.

We concluded this visit to Palestine by visiting the Temple of Jerusalem and several mosques. Then back to Tel Aviv with a visit to St. Peter's Church in Joppa where St. Peter explained a vision that he had about his call to ministry to the Gentiles (Act.11:7ff).

Before returning home, we took a side trip to Istanbul, which dates back to 600 B.C. There we said Mass in the Church of St. Anthony and visited the city by bus, admiring such places as the mosques, the Basilica of St. Sophia, the Imperial Palace of the Topkapi Museum, and the Great Bazaar.

The following day we took a boat ride on the Bosphorus Strait. This strait forms the boundary between Europe and Asia. We also went by ferry to the Asiatic side of Istanbul and finally up a mountain for a scenic view of the city.

My trip to the Holy Land was like a dream come true. It was not a tourist trip but rather a spiritual adventure much like a retreat. I am grateful to God for this opportunity.

The only sad feature about the pilgrimage to the Holy Land was to witness the effects of the bitter Six Day War. This was the war of June 5–11, 1967. It was also called the Arab-Israeli War. On our arrival in Tel Aviv, as we exited the plane we saw Israeli soldiers on the roof of the terminal building with machine guns in hand. We were to stay in the Arab part of Jerusalem with an Arab chauffeur to take us around. There were several checkpoints on our journeys and in some cases we heard heated exchanges between our driver and the Israeli soldiers. The fact that one of the priests in the car was wearing a traditional Arab keffiyeh did not help matters. The age-old hostility was still very much in evidence and has not gone away since.

Another example of this took place after my visit of the Dead Sea Scrolls in the Rockefeller Museum in New Jerusalem. I hailed a cab to take me back to the Jerusalem Gate in Old Jerusalem. The cab driver was an Israeli. When I told him where I was going, he told me: "Not in this cab. I'm not taking any chances driving into that neighborhood. You find yourself an Arab cab driver." I remembered the words of the Psalmist: "Pray for the peace of Jerusalem." (Ps. 122:6)

Eucharistic Congress, South Korea
September 25–October 9, 1989

With a group of pilgrims from British Columbia we departed for the 44th International Congress in South Korea. We made a first stop in Singapore where we said Mass in the Cathedral of the Good Shepherd and met the Archbishop. We toured this small island of 2½ million people by day in a chartered bus. In the evening we enjoyed a twilight dinner cruise along the harbor. We were also treated to a colorful multi-racial cultural show in the hotel.

We visited Sentosa Island just off the coast of Singapore. In

Malay it means "Isle of Tranquility" and it well deserves the name. It was used as a military base during World War II. Another notable sight was the Jurong Bird Park with its three thousand exotic, colorful and rare birds. We were given a nostalgic tour of old Singapore in a trishaw—a one-man pedal-powered vehicle.

A featured event was our trip to Malaysia, where we said Mass in the Church of St. Francis Xavier in Malacca, a city of about 300,000 people. Between the years 1545 and 1552, St. Francis visited Malacca five times and built churches and schools there. He translated the catechism into the Malay language. St. Francis died at Sancian Island off the coast of China at the age of forty-six. His body was brought back to Malacca and was buried in St. Paul's Hill Church for six months. Later his body was taken to Goa. It was in St. Paul's Church that St. Francis Xavier preached and prayed. His empty tomb in the church is the most ancient relic in the Far East. The building of a new church in Malacca dedicated to St. Francis Xavier was begun in 1849.

On October 1, we flew to Hong Kong. Our pilgrimate was nine years before Hong Kong reverted from Great Britain to the People's Republic of China. We spent a few days visiting this beautiful city. We celebrated Mass in English in the Church of the Holy Rosary.

On October 3 we took a trip by hovercraft to visit three cities in Red China. The first was Shekou. There we boarded a chartered bus with a Chinese driver. We tried to ask him questions about the uprisings and massacres in Tiananmen Square on May 19 and June 4, 1989. He would say nothing for fear of being reported.

The city of Shekou had about 50,000 people. It is the first special economic zone in China. But you would never know it. Among other things, we visited an open market where we saw men and women arriving there in rusted old bicycles to purchase food. The food was displayed in very unsanitary fashion. The whole place looked so primitive. The merchants still used old hand-held scales. The people looked so sad.

From there we took a catamaran across the Pearl River to the city of Zhuhai. It is the nearest border city to the island of Macau. We passed through an old village town with duck farms, buffaloes and, of course, rice fields. In Zhuhai we were treated to an extremely elegant lunch in a five-star hotel. I had never seen such a gorgeous restaurant before. The décor was exceptional and the display of foods was unbelievable. It was quite a contrast from the marketplace in Shekou.

Our next stop was to the city of Zhongshan, the birthplace of the founder of the Republic of China. We visited the former residence of Dr. Sun Yat-sen and the Memorial School erected in his memory. The school was absolutely first class. We toured several of the buildings and classrooms. It was a holiday in China so there was little activity on campus—except for the library. There we saw many students poring over their books. They were not in the least distracted by this group of Western tourists walking in on them. They were so absorbed in their studies. We were told that only the brightest students from all of China were admitted to the school.

Our last stop was a trip by high-speed hovercraft to the island of Macau, about forty miles from Hong Kong. Macau was then a territory under Portuguese administration; the Portuguese ceded the territory to the People's Republic of China in 1999. Macau, with its dense population of about half a million people, is the place where East and West meet. It has been the oldest European settlement in Asia for over four hundred years. Macau is famous for its luxurious casinos. We had no interest in casinos. We spent our time visiting the ruins of St. Paul's Church and the Temple of Kun Yam.

We were back in Hong Kong after a whirlwind visit. Now, the real purpose of our trip began—the Eucharistic Congress. On October 4 we flew to Seoul, Korea and attended evening Mass in the beautiful Gothic cathedral of Myongdong. The cathedral parish has over thirty thousand members and every month there are between three to four hundred adult baptisms. South Korea has a population of about 43 million, 10 million of whom live in the city of Seoul. About half of the South Korean population is Buddhist while the other half is Christian. Of the Christians, over two million are Catholic. Half of these are between the ages of twenty and forty, having been baptized within the last seven or eight years. South Korea is truly a young and vibrant faith community.

The theme of the Congress was "Christ, our Peace". The purpose was to pray for the peaceful unification of South and North Korea. The logo of the Congress was a broken circle with a cross in the center. When we registered for the Congress, we were given a packet of information on the events of the Congress as well as a laminated copy of the logo which we wore around our necks at all times.

On October 5 we went to the opening Mass of the Congress in the Olympic Gymnastics Hall, which was filled to capacity. On the evening of the same day, all the bishops and priests in attendance were invited by various Catholic Korean families to celebrate the *agape*, which is a prayer service and family meal. Two of us were guests in the

With companion Fr. Ponti in Korean family home for "agape" meal.

home of a married couple and their children. The couple were both medical doctors with a son who was studying in California. The evening included Scriptural readings both in English and Korean, silent meditation, and songs. The meal consisted of a fine variety of Korean foods. It was so inspiring to witness the deep faith of this family. These people were so gracious that they offered to pick us up early on the morning of our departure and drive us to the airport.

On October 6 we celebrated Mass at the Chol Tu San Martyrs' Shrine. This shrine is situated on a small rocky mountain next to the Han River. During the cruel persecution of Byong-In in 1866, Catholics were beheaded on the top of the hill and their bodies thrown into the Han River. For about two years, thousands of Christians were executed in this way. The people began to call the mountain "Chol Tu San" which means "The Beheading Hill". Many of these martyrs were canonized by Pope John Paul II in his first visit to Seoul in 1984.

An interesting thing happened one day. A priest friend and I took a walk through the narrow streets of the shopping district of Seoul. As we passed one store, a young man about 20–25 years of age saw us with the Congress logo around our necks. He asked us if we were Catholics. When we said "yes", a big smile came over his face and he yelled: "Me Catoric too", and in full view of merchants and bystanders he made the Sign of the Cross. Obviously he was very proud of his faith and was not ashamed to show it even in a heavily non-Christian environment.

One evening the two of us went for a vigil service in the Jamsil Gymnasium. There were 35,000 people present, mainly young Koreans.

The prayers, songs and presentations were all in Korean. When we arrived, one of the ushers came to us to apologize that everything was in Korean. She said the program was intended for Koreans and not visitors but we were welcome to stay. We did and enjoyed the enthusiasm of those young people. The vigil lasted throughout the night and concluded with a dawn Mass at 6:00 a.m.

On October 7 my priest companion and I went to the cathedral and were in the square when the Angelus bells rang. People were scurrying to and fro in the square. To our amazement, when the Angelus bells rang, many (presumably Catholic) people in the square stopped and remained motionless as statues as they recited the Angelus prayer. We had never seen anything like that. We were told that it was a general practice every day at noon in the cathedral square.

By this time, Pope John Paul II arrived in Korea, and at 2:00 p.m. he presided at a Holy Hour for the clergy and religious. We numbered about one thousand. The service took place in the Nonhyon-Dong parish church in the evening, from 5:30 to 8:30. It was such a privilege for us bishops to concelebrate Mass for the young people attending the Congress.

The highlight of the whole Congress took place on Sunday, October 8 with the Solemn Mass of the Eucharistic Congress in the Youido Plaza. There were an estimated one million people present, mostly Asians. The Mass lasted three hours but nobody really noticed. What a privilege for us bishops to concelebrate Mass with the Pope on this solemn occasion. As we exited the plaza after Mass, one Japanese lady bowed to us in typical Asian style and said: "You have honored us by your presence". And I said to myself: "It's the other way around. We have been honored by your presence and your praiseworthy witness of faith."

On the following day, we celebrated our very last Mass in Korea at the Catholic Martyrs Memorial Church of Saenamto. This beautiful new church, built in traditional Korean architectural style, was completed in 1987, just two years before the Congress. It was built on the spot where the first native Korean priest, St. Andrew Kim, was beheaded in 1801 together with 102 other martyrs. After Mass we visited the museum of the Korean martyrs in the church. Our guides were young Koreans who displayed with great pride the many artifacts belonging to St. Andrew Kim. Judging from the rapid growth of the Church in Korea, that old saying is true: "The blood of the martyrs is the seed of the Church."

Pilgrimage to Europe with Kamloops priests September 5–17, 1990

On September 5, five of our Kamloops priests and I left for Europe headed for Munich, Germany. My brother Joe and I had been to Munich in 1952 not long after World War II when the city and its once-beautiful cathedral were in total ruin. But now, thirty-eight years later, the city and its cathedral were restored to their pristine beauty.

One of our first visits in Munich was to the former Nazi concentration camp in Dachau. Between March of 1933 and April of 1945, two hundred thousand prisoners passed through the Dachau camp and its branch camps. There, over 32,000 died through torture, execution, hunger or epidemics. This once beautiful 1,200-year-old town of Dachau became synonymous with Nazi terror. Since then the German government built a memorial on the site of the former concentration camp. In the museum there are photos and graphic details of all that took place there during those infamous years. There are several blocks in the museum with a description of what they were used for. Block 26, for example, was called "Priesterblock" where many priests were imprisoned and eventually executed. On the walls were pictures of some of them. We were shown a real-life documentary with photos of the atrocities which took place there. Seated beside us during the showing was a group of young German college students. When the film was over, there was a deathly silence in the room. I felt so sorry for those German students who left the room quietly with heads bowed, ashamed of what they had seen. They cannot be held responsible for the sins of their forefathers.

After our visit to the museum we went to Oberammergau on September 6 and were billeted in the home of a kind Bavarian family. They felt so honored to have a bishop and five Canadian priests staying with them.

The next morning, we went to see the world famous decennial Passion Play in an open-air stage. The play was presented in two parts: a morning session of two and a half hours, and three hours after lunch. The Passion Play is a stirring, world renowned drama that has for more than three centuries commemorated Christ's last days on earth. It began as the fulfillment of a vow to God on the part of one hundred citizens of Oberammergau who were spared from the bubonic plague in the seventeenth century. All the actors and actresses are cast not so much on sheer acting ability but on the basis of their good morals and character. Those not born in Oberammergau must have lived there for at least twenty years before being accepted in the cast. It was truly a powerful drama.

The following day we took the train to Lyons, France. In Lyons we visited St. John's Cathedral, which dates back to the fifteenth century. Lyons is the place where two ecumenical councils were held.

On September 9 we went to the town of Ars, made famous by the 41-year ministry of St. John Vianney, known as the Curé of Ars. We went there because St. John Vianney is the secondary patron of the Diocese of Kamloops and patron of parish priests. We went to the church to celebrate Mass. When the sacristan learned that I was a bishop from Canada with five priests, he gave us the red carpet treatment. He took us down to the crypt where we celebrated Mass on the original altar used by St. John. We also used his chalice and wore his vestments. What a thrill! I even sat down for a few minutes in his original confessional and said to myself: "Anyone who could sit for hours on that very hard oak bench deserves to be declared a saint."

When St. John Vianney was assigned to Ars in 1818, it was a little town of three hundred people. The original church was a small building with a single nave measuring about 35 feet by 15 feet. The sanctuary had just about enough room for the altar. Today, the new church is a large basilica.

We read in his biography that when St. John Vianney was assigned to Ars, he was on his way to the town when a huge fog caused him to lose sight of the village. A young boy came along and showed him the path to follow. On a small mountain overlooking the town of Ars, there is a beautiful monument of the boy pointing St. John Vianney in the direction of Ars. On the monument there are inscribed the words which St. John Vianney said to the boy when he met him: "You show me the way to Ars and I will show you the way to heaven." That young lad died on August 7, 1859, just three days after the death of St. John Vianney. A prophecy fulfilled?

Our next visit was to the Shrine of Our Lady of Lourdes. We arrived in the evening of September 10 in time to take part in the beautiful candlelight procession. People from around the world recited the Rosary and sang the "Lourdes Hymn" in their own languages. It was very inspiring.

The next morning it was a huge privilege for me to be the main celebrant at the Mass in the Lourdes grotto at 7:30 a.m. This is the spot where the Blessed Virgin Mary appeared to St. Bernadette. In the evening we saw a movie on the life of St. Bernadette. It reminded me so much of the movie I had seen as a boy, *The Song of Bernadette*, with Jennifer Jones' Oscar-winning performance as Bernadette.

From Lourdes we went to visit the city of Marseille on the coast of France. We said Mass in the beautiful Church of Notre Dame de la Garde. This church is located on a hill overlooking the Mediterranean. The place was once a fortress. We also wanted to venerate the body of St. Eugene de Mazenod, founder of the Oblates of Mary Immaculate, members of which had been serving in the Diocese of Kamloops for many years. It was early afternoon and the church where his body is laid was closed. Bad timing on our part; it was siesta time.

We finally made our way to Rome to take part in the Worldwide Retreat for Priests in the Paul VI Audience Hall in Vatican City from September 14–18. The theme was "Called to Evangelize" in anticipation of the year 2000. There were a number of renowned speakers who conducted the retreat, notably people like Mother Teresa of Calcutta, Sr. Briege McKenna from Ireland, Cardinal Jaime Sin of Manila, Fr. Tom Forrest, coordinator of the retreat, Molly Scanlon Kelly, and many others.

On the last day of the retreat, the retreatants took part in a solemn procession from the papal audience hall to the Basilica of St. Peter for the concluding liturgy. The presiding celebrant and homilist was none other than His Holiness John Paul II. What a wonderful way to conclude this very inspirational retreat and our pilgrimage to Europe.

Pilgrimage to the Philippines and Australia January 1995

After a stopover in Taipei, I arrived in Manila on January 7 where I was welcomed by my Scalabrinian confreres from Quezon City. On January 10, I was taken to visit Smokey Mountain, which at the time was the city's garbage dump. Here many people of all ages gathered to await the arrival of the garbage trucks to see what they could salvage for their survival. Fortunately Smokey Mountain no longer exists. We visited the Canossian Fathers, who staff the parish of San Pablo in the city of Tondo. This is an extremely poor community of over 100,000 parishioners with an attached mission of 45,000 more. I truly admired the zeal of those two priests living and ministering in the midst of such abject poverty.

We saw a completely different side of life when we visited Makati in Metro Manila. Makati is the financial capital of the Philippines and the street that runs through the heart of downtown is called the

"Wall Street of the Philippines". Makati is one of the most modern cities in the Philippines with its GT International Tower and several five-star hotels. What a contrast from Tondo!

We also drove to the area that was devastated by the eruption of Mount Pinatubo in June 1991. Eight hundred people were killed and 100,000 left homeless because of the eruption. As we drove on these miles of ash, we saw some chimneys barely surfacing above the ash.

During my days in the Philippines, I stayed with our Scalabrinian community in the outskirts of Quezon City. I was most grateful to Fr. Bruno Ciceri, c.s. for giving me such an interesting tour of those various places.

Finally, on January 12, Pope John Paul II arrived in Manila for the World Youth Day, which was the main reason for my pilgrimage. On the following day, the young people conducted an impressive Way of the Cross. Delegates from more than one hundred countries participated in the event dressed in their native costumes. On the evening of January 14, the Holy Father had an exhilarating session with thousands of young people in Luneta Park. It was so nice to see the Holy Father interacting with the youth in such a joyful way.

The following day, Sunday, January 15, was the most impressive day I have ever experienced in my life. It was the closing Liturgy of the 1995 World Youth Day. Surrounding the Pope around the Quirino grandstand were thirty-five Cardinals, about three hundred bishops, two thousand priests and an estimated five million people. Some have said that this was the largest gathering of people for a single event in the history of humanity. All this mass of people jammed the Rizal Park and the surrounding area. The Holy Father could not make it through the crowd in the Popemobile so he was flown to the grandstand in the presidential helicopter. The cardinals and bishops had the same problem. Our bus could not take us to the trailers where we were to vest for Mass. So we had to walk with much difficulty through that sea of people. The Mass started late and lasted three hours. However, the ceremonies were so inspiring that the time went by quickly. At the end of Mass when the Pope was saying his goodbye, three hundred doves were symbolically released and the Holy Father gave his final exhortation to the youth in eleven different languages. Truly, it was a weekend to remember.

I decided to follow the Holy Father to Sydney, Australia, for the beatification of the first native-born Australian, Mary McKillop. This event took place in a race track with 250,000 people present. They looked like a handful as compared to the five million in Manila. But it was a beautiful ceremony and a milestone in the history of Australia. On Sunday, January 22, I flew to Melbourne and visited the place where Blessed Mary McKillop was born, as well as the museum displaying her heroic life story in film. Eventually I made my way back home to Canada reflecting on all the moving experiences I had during this graced period.

Pilgrimage to Europe #2
July 7–31, 2008

On July 7 I left for Rome with two of my Scalabrinian confreres, Fr. Gino Dalpiaz and Fr. Vince Cutrara. We were able to make this pilgrimage thanks to the generosity of a kind benefactor from New York. We began our pilgrimage in the Eternal City of Rome where we stopped to pray in all four of the major basilicas.

On July 10, we flew to Lourdes where we joined a group of pilgrims from Ampleforth Abbey in England. These consisted of the abbot, several English priests and about eighty disabled people. There was also a very large number of young volunteers who looked after the disabled for the entire time of the pilgrimage. We were so impressed with the spirit of those young people who sacrificed vacation time to perform such a Christian service. We took part in all the usual activities: the candlelight procession; Benediction of the Blessed Sacrament; quiet prayer in the Tent of Adoration; the river walk; and especially the Masses in the Grotto.

This pilgrimage to Lourdes on the sesquicentennial anniversary of the first apparition of the Blessed Virgin to St. Bernadette was particularly meaningful to me. My first visit there was as a newly ordained priest in July of 1957. I had gone there to place my whole priesthood under the protection of the Blessed Virgin Mary. As a young priest I had no idea what lay ahead of me.

Now on this special occasion, I was again in Lourdes to thank the Blessed Mother for her guidance in these fifty-one years of my priesthood. In all honesty, it was a great ride and I could not have done it without her. I learned the value of that famous prayer we used to recite in the seminary: "Remember, O most gracious Virgin Mary, that never was it known that anyone who fled to your protection or sought your intercession was left unaided." How true!

On July 18 we flew to Lisbon where we visited the Church of St. Anthony of Padua and the home where he was born in the latter part of the twelfth century. This miracle worker was my mother's favorite saint so I was eager to visit the place of his birth. I was very impressed with the devotion the people of Lisbon had for this saint: the square and the cafés all named after St. Anthony. I said to one person: "I see you people have a great devotion to St. Anthony of Padua." He immediately corrected me: "You mean St. Anthony of Lisbon." The Italians were not going to steal their saint.

From Lisbon we took a bus to the Shrine of Our Lady of Fatima, where the Blessed Virgin appeared to three young shepherds named Lucia, Jacinta and Francisco. We visited the homes where they were born and their tombs in the basilica. We said Mass in the chapel on the site of the apparitions. We prayed the Way of the Cross on a hill nearby and took part in the evening candlelight procession.

On July 27 we eventually found our way back to Rome. On the following day, I visited Archbishop Velasio de Paolis, a Scalabrinian confrere and friend. He was formerly professor of canon law at the Gregorian University and now Prefect of the Economic Affairs of the Holy See. He offered to take the three of us by car to visit Assisi, the town made famous by St. Francis. We visited all the holy places. Assisi is such a remarkable place.

Eventually we made our way back to Chicago on July 31.

A Pilgrimage Unfulfilled

Whenever a bishop is consecrated who does not have a diocese of his own, he is given a titular diocese that is no longer in existence. When I was named auxiliary bishop of Vancouver, I was given the titular see of Nasai in North Africa, now known as Tunisia. I was excited by this because one of my favorite saints was St. Augustine who was born in North Africa. He was converted to Christianity after a not-too-exemplary youth. For thirty years, his mother, St. Monica, prayed that he would be converted and receive baptism. Augustine went to Milan where he visited the famous cathedral and heard the Archbishop, St. Ambrose, deliver a sermon that moved him to embrace Christianity. Augustine was baptized by St. Ambrose in the cathedral of Milan on Easter Sunday of the year 387 A.D. Augustine became a priest and later Bishop of Hippo in North Africa.

Augustine was a voluminous writer and one of the greatest theologians in the Church. His book *Confessions* is still quite popular and I read it several times, especially the parts about his loving relationship as bishop with his mother at the time of her death. He was very much in my thoughts when, in like manner, I was with my mother at her death and celebrated her funeral as bishop. In my homily, I quoted the words of St. Augustine: "We did not think it fitting to solemnize that funeral with tearful cries and groans...she did not die in misery nor did she meet with total death. This we knew by sure evidence and proofs given by her good life and by her unfeigned faith . . ." (*Confessions,* p. 224). In his prayer to God about his mother, Augustine wrote: "She desired only to be remembered at your altar, which she had served without the loss of a single day." (ibid, p. 228) Thank God for devout mothers.

In recent years, the actual baptistry where Augustine was baptized by Ambrose was discovered beneath the Gothic masterpiece that is the Duomo of Milan. In my trips to Milan, I made it a point to visit the excavations and pause in prayer at the baptistry. I also said Mass several times in the chapel of the Duomo below the main altar where the body of St. Charles Borromeo, patron of the Scalabrinian community, is entombed.

Augustine died in 430 A.D. His relics were transferred to Pavia and placed in an urn in the Basilica of San Pietro in Ciel d'Oro. I was able to visit the basilica and saw on the floor a portion of a mosaic from the ancient Cathedral of Hippo where Augustine was bishop for thirty-five years. It was my desire to visit my titular diocese of Nasai and recall the days in the fourth century when Christianity was a flourishing community until the invasion of the Vandals. Unfortunately, I never made it to North Africa. Nor was I able to visit the region of Nasai or Hippo where Augustine ministered but I was pleased to pray where his body lies at rest.

You are Peter
and upon this
rock I will build
my church.

(Mt 16:18)

JESUS entrusted to Peter the keys of the Kingdom of Heaven. While Christ will always remain the invisible head of the Church, Peter becomes the visible head. Every Pope is a successor of Peter, just as every bishop is the successor of the apostles under the leadership of the pope.

On the day of my consecration as bishop I publicly pledged loyalty and obedience to the pope as the successor of Peter. Throughout my life as bishop, I endeavored to keep this promise to the best of my ability. For this reason it was always a joy and a privilege for me to meet and converse with the Holy Father.

Two of the most solemn papal ceremonies in Rome were the beatifications and the canonizations of new saints. Everyone in life needs positive role models. The saints are our role models. My first presence at a beatification was in 1953 when I was *caudatario* of Cardinal Piazza. The new blessed was a religious sister named Bertilla Boscardin who was later canonized by Pope John XXIII in 1961.

On May 29, 1954, I was fortunate to be among the crowd at St. Peter's Basilica when Pope Pius XII canonized St. Pius X. The following day (Sunday) I walked in procession when the body of the new saint was being carried through the streets from St. Peter's Basilica to the Basilica of St. Mary Major. Later that same year, I had occasion to visit the town of Riese where the new saint was born and the parish church where he was baptized. I held St. Pius X in high esteem because of his interest in liturgy and the reform of Church music.

A few weeks later, June 2, I was again *caudatario* of Cardinal Piazza when Pope Pius XII canonized five new saints, one of whom was the young boy Dominic Savio, a pupil of St. John Bosco. I had read the life of Dominic Savio in the minor seminary and was so honored to be present at his canonization.

As bishop, I was again privileged to be present in St. Peter's Square on October 11, 1998, when Pope John Paul II canonized the Carmelite Sister Teresa Benedicta of the Cross, also known as Edith Stein. Sister Teresa Benedicta was put to death by the Nazis in the gas chamber in Auschwitz in 1942 because she was Jewish. Pope John Paul II referred to the new saint as "an eminent daughter of Israel and a faithful daughter of the Church."

On October 19, 2003, Mother Teresa of Calcutta was beatified in Rome and I was privileged to take part in the ceremony. I had met Mother Teresa in Vancouver in 1976 when she came there to address the United Nations International Habitat Conference. Archbishop Carney wanted to take advantage of her presence in Vancouver to address the Catholic community of the archdiocese. She graciously accepted. The program was held in the Pacific Colosseum. Almost twenty thousand people came out to hear her. I was introduced to Mother Teresa by the Archbishop. He asked me to give the invocation before her address Naturally, I felt honored to do so. I had read her book *Something Beautiful for God*, which impressed me. The theme of her message to the crowd in the Colosseum was poverty. She did discuss the kind of poverty one sees in the poorer countries where people are starving to death and abandoned in the streets. But she also pointed to the poverty in Canada and the United States, where children are aborted at will. She alluded to the U.S. Supreme Court decision Roe *vs.* Wade of just a few years before. She emphasized the sacredness of human life from conception to the time of natural death. In her mind, a country that aborts its children is a poor country in a more profound sense of the word. This is the woman who in 1992 was awarded the Nobel Peace Prize. She has gone to her eternal reward but the community of the Sisters of Charity still lives on. The Sisters continue to minister to the poor and the abandoned in 123 countries including Russia, Albania (Mother Teresa's native land) and Cuba.

Bishop John Baptist Scalabrini would also one day join the ranks of the blessed after years of prayer by Scalabrinian priests and religious brothers and sisters throughout the world. There were many events leading up to this great day. The first that I personally participated in happened on September 9, 1986, when the Scalabrinians sponsored an International Conference on Scalabrini in Rome. I was honored to be celebrant and homilist at the opening Mass. On the following day, I was invited to deliver a paper on "The Spirituality of Bishop Scalabrini." In doing my research for the address I was convinced more and more that this apostolic man would one day be declared blessed and later a saint. He was truly an extraordinary person and we are proud to honor him as our founder. At the conclusion of the conference, the Holy Father received us in audience.

The following year was a banner year for all Scalabrinians. It marked the centennial anniversary of the foundation of the community. Celebrations were held in all parts of the Scalabrinian world. On October 10, I was invited to concelebrate Mass with Cardinal O'Connor in St. Patrick's Cathedral in New York. I was very impressed by the cardinal's homily wherein he expressed a knowledge and appreciation of the person of Bishop Scalabrini.

The long-awaited day of the founder's beatification finally arrived. On November 8, 1997, several bishops (including four Scalabrinians), hundreds of Scalabrinian priests, sisters and lay missionaries, together with thousands of people from all parts of the Scalabrinian world converged on Rome. The ceremonies began that evening with a multilingual prayer vigil in the Basilica of St. Paul Outside the Walls. The atmosphere was electrifying.

The following day, to accommodate the huge crowd, the beatification ceremony took place outdoors in St. Peter's Square. We Scalabrinian bishops had the privilege of concelebrating Mass with Pope John Paul II. Everyone listened attentively to the Pope's decree of beatification outlining the virtues of this saintly man. Shouts of joy came forth from the whole crowd when the huge tapestry of Bishop Scalabrini was unfurled on the façade of the basilica. After Mass we bishops had a chance to greet the Holy Father personally and to thank him for this great honor to our community (photographs, p. 160).

The following day, because of the rain, we had our final meeting with the Pope in the hall of benediction. It was time to say goodbye to the Holy Father and to one another as we departed to the four ends of the earth. It was a weekend to remember.

I never had the privilege of privately meeting Pope John Paul II's successor, Benedict XVI. However, I did meet him twice when he was Cardinal Joseph Ratzinger, Prefect of the Congregation of the Doctrine of the Faith.

The first time occurred on February 6–10, 1984, in Dallas, Texas. The Knights of Columbus sponsored a Symposium for the bishops of the United States, Canada, Mexico and the Philippines. The topic was "Medico-Moral Problems." Cardinal Ratzinger was invited to attend. He sat in on all the sessions of that week-long seminar and listened intently to all the presentations. At the breaks, he would socialize with the bishops and showed himself to be a very congenial person. On the final day, he was asked to make some comments on the talks he heard. He gave a most brilliant summary of all the presentations. All the bishops were impressed, and I told him so.

The second time was in November of 1988 on the occasion of

my *ad limina* visit to the Holy Father, John Paul II. During that time it is customary for bishops to visit some of the Roman congregations. A few of us bishops from British Columbia decided to go to the Congregation of the Doctrine of the Faith. Cardinal Ratzinger personally welcomed us very graciously. He answered our theological concerns with great clarity and kindness and did not at all appear to be defensive or authoritarian. I was deeply impressed and could not understand why he was presented so poorly in the media. Expressions such as "the Pope's Rottweiler" certainly did not seem to fit. Even the stray cats of Rome appreciated his gentleness as they accompanied him frequently on his walk from his apartment to his office. Pope Benedict XVI was very gracious towards me. On the occasion of my fiftieth anniversary of priestly ordination on March 19, 2007, he was kind enough to send me an autographed message of congratulations in Latin with his photo thanking me for my service to the Church. (See back cover.)

It was my pleasure to meet John XXIII in an audience shortly after he was elected pope. After five years as pope, "Good Pope John" was succeed by Paul VI. I never met Pope Paul VI because he died just three weeks after naming me bishop. Giovanni Battista Montini was Archbishop of Milan when Pope John XXIII was elected to succeed Pope Pius XII. One of the new Pope's first official acts was to name Archbishop Montini a cardinal. You know the rest of the story. Paul VI's successor, Pope John Paul I, was pope for only thirty-three days. It was his successor, Pope John Paul II, who transferred me from Auxiliary Bishop of Vancouver to Bishop of Kamloops.

My first meeting with Pope John Paul II took place in February of 1981 when the pope returned from an historic papal visit to Japan. He made a brief stopover in Anchorage, Alaska. Archbishop Carney and I decided to fly to Anchorage to greet him. We had the privilege of concelebrating Mass with the pope in an open field together with a few cardinals and bishops. After Mass we were able to greet the pope personally and exchange a few words. I was surprised to see how many people gathered out in the open to attend the pope's Mass. I was also surprised to see the large number of Native Americans who slept in the park the night before just to get a better glimpse of the pope. An outdoor Mass in late February in Alaska? Who would have "thunk" it?

Every five years, each bishop in charge of a diocese makes a very important visit to Rome. It is called the *ad limina* visit, meaning "to the threshold" of St. Peter in Rome. This visit includes a private

"I remember you."

audience with the Holy Father. However, six months prior to the visit, the bishop must send to Rome a very detailed report about the status of his diocese. The pope is then briefed about the report and may address some issues in the private audience.

My first such visit was in October of 1983. As I sat down next to Pope John Paul II in his study, he had a large map of Canada on his desk and he said to me: "I remember you. You are from Kamloops." He then pointed to Kamloops on the map. Knowing that a significant part of my ministry was with the First Nations People, he asked me several questions about them and asked how the Church was responding to their needs. The audience lasted twenty minutes and I was so proud when the Holy Father asked me to have a photo taken of the two of us. I got plenty of mileage from that photo and made it into a Christmas card for family and friends.

The following year, in September of 1984, Pope John Paul II made his pastoral visit to Canada and he came to Vancouver. For us Western Canadian bishops, the highlight was the Papal Mass that the bishops of British Columbia concelebrated with him in the presence of several hundred thousand people in the airport of Abbotsford. The bishops vested for Mass in a trailer before processing to the huge grandstand. A few of us were standing outside the trailer when the Holy Father stopped by to greet us. When he came to me he said: "Ah, here is that young pastoral bishop from Kamloops." He may have remembered me from my visit the year before. I was quite flattered by that comment because aren't all bishops pastoral by nature?

We were flown by military helicopter to Vancouver. It was my first trip on a helicopter, and the forty-mile flight to Vancouver was much more pleasant than those on the small single engine planes. Then again, there were several bishops aboard, so how risky could it be? Interestingly, my second helicopter ride was also associated with Pope John Paul II because it took place in 1995 when I went to Australia for the papal visit. One of my confreres, Fr. Nevio Capra, c.s., founder of several Scalabrinian Villages in Australia, had a friend who was a commercial helicopter pilot. The friend took us on a tour of the city of Sydney and its scenic harbor. While in Sydney, I stayed with the Scalabrinian Provincial of Australia, Fr. Domenico Ceresoli. January 25th was his birthday, so we celebrated it by going to see Giacomo Puccini's opera *Turandot* in the elegant Sydney Opera House.

Now let's go back to Pope John Paul's visit to Vancouver. When our helicopter landed in Vancouver, we were driven to B.C. Place to attend a special program entitled "A Celebration of Life" with the bishops seated next to the Holy Father. The pope seemed to enjoy this colorful folklore presentation. After the performance, the Holy Father and the British Columbia bishops had dinner together in the cathedral rectory. The pope was his usual pleasant self although he showed some signs of weariness after such a long day.

My next *ad limina* visit took place in November of 1988. The bishops always go to the visit by region and this was the time for the Western bishops of Canada. The visit began with a concelebrated Mass with the Pope in his private chapel at 7:00 a.m. My audience with him took place at 11:30 a.m., after which we were invited to lunch in the Pope's dining room. There were about twelve of us. Respecting the bilingual nature of Canada, during the meal the Pope spoke half the time in French and the other half in English. He had no problem answering our questions. At the conclusion of the visit the pope gave us his final address and said goodbye to each of us.

The next quinquennial visit of the Western Canadian Bishops was in September of 1993. This meeting was not held in the Vatican but in the Pope's summer residence in Castelgandolfo, a small town overlooking Lago Albano about twenty miles southeast of Rome.

We arrived in Rome on September 13. The following day I had my private audience at 11:45am. This would prove to be my last and most memorable meeting with Pope John Paul II. After we finished the official business, I ventured to ask the pope: "Holy Father, may I respectfully talk to you about a personal matter?" He moved back from the table and looked perplexed, not knowing what to expect. I told him that I had served in Canada for twenty-two years and humbly asked if he would accept my resignation so I could return back home to the States. The reason was that I had spent most of my life in Europe, New York, and British Columbia and never really got to know my family very well. I still had a brother and sister living in Chicago and would like to spend more time with them. The pope's reply was quick and to the point. He said: "And don't you think I would like to go back to Poland?" A great one-liner. However, he was kind enough to leave the door open. He said that if this desire persisted, I should pray about it, think about it and then talk to the nuncio in Ottawa. He did not dismiss the request completely.

On September 16, we left Rome again for Castelgandolfo where we concelebrated Mass in the Pope's private chapel. We took a walk around the beautiful papal gardens. At 12:00 noon we assembled once again to hear the pope's address about the state of the Church in Western Canada, wherein he offered some pastoral recommendations. At 2:00 p.m., we had lunch with the pope in his dining room and much to my embarrassment the bishops insisted that I sit to the immediate right of the pope. In light of our conversation of a few days earlier, I knew that the pope would not hold that against me. He did not. He was very pleasant. In any case, you can be sure that I was very conscious about my table etiquette.

I took plenty of time to pray and think about the idea of retirement. I did not want to act too hastily on the pope's suggestion about retirement. We were in the midst of preparing two important historic events that were to take place in the diocese.

The first was the first-ever Kamloops Diocesan Synod. I had already officially proclaimed the convocation of the Synod "Journey in Faith" on December 22, 1991. This was the 46th anniversary of the founding of the Diocese (Appendix One). The whole diocese was to take an active role in the process, which took four years to complete. The formal synod itself took place at the Immaculate Heart of Mary Retreat House on October 22–26, 1995, with forty delegates from across the diocese and a facilitator. After gathering all the deliberations from the various committees, it was my task to summarize them in a post-synodal letter that took a few months to complete.

The second important event was the fiftieth anniversary of the foundation of the Kamloops Diocese. In anticipation of this historic milestone, several celebrations were held in the various pastoral zones in the diocese. The solemn liturgical climax took place on Christmas Eve, December 24, 1995, in the new Riverside Colosseum. All the priests of the diocese concelebrated Mass with me. The religious sisters of the diocese were there. A total of almost five thousand people attended. The atmosphere was one of great emotion.

In his Apostolic Letter "Tertio Millenio Adveniente" of November 1994, Pope John Paul II invited all the faithful to prepare for the coming of the new millenium. In 1996 a Diocesan Pastoral Council was formed of representatives of the three pastoral zones of the diocese. One of their suggestions for the three years of preparation for the coming of the Great Jubilee of the year 2000 was that I write a monthly homily in the form of a brief pastoral letter. This letter was to be read at all the parishes and missions of the diocese. The priests did not mind at all because on that Sunday they did not have to prepare a homily. (Appendix Two).

When the diocesan celebrations were completed, I felt it was the time to take up the pope's suggestion and discuss further my request for retirement. I flew to Ottawa in February of 1997 and presented my case to the apostolic nuncio. He said he would do all he could to further my cause but apparently for some reason my request did not reach the pope's desk. The whole matter lay dormant for a while. In the meantime, Cardinal Bernardin Gantin, Prefect of the Congregation of Bishops, who was the one to process my request, retired. He was succeeded by Cardinal Lucas Moreiro Neves, a Brazilian Dominican. I happened to be in Rome in October of 1998 and decided to speak personally to Cardinal Neves about my request. We met in his office for over two hours and he promised me that as soon as he could, he would speak directly to the Holy Father about this matter. I was not totally unknown to Cardinal Neves because when I was proposed as bishop in 1978 he was secretary to the Cardinal of the Congregation and was familiar with my dossier. On July 9, 1999, I received a letter from the Cardinal informing me that the Holy Father was willing to accept my resignation. As per proper protocol, I wrote a formal written request to the pope. The reply I received stated that the official date of my retirement would be September 3, 1999.

However, the kindly Pope John Paul II did not forget me. He held no grudge against me for bailing out of Kamloops prematurely. (Bishops must submit their retirement at age 75. I was only 69.) On the occasion of the twenty-fifth anniversary of my consecration as bishop, on September 21, 2003, Pope John Paul II sent me a parchment with his photo and a message in Latin thanking me for my ministry as bishop, especially among the First Nations People. He personally autographed the document. (See back cover.)

On the morning of September 3, 1999, the day of the announcement of my resignation, I scheduled a meeting in Kamloops with the diocesan consultors. I gave them the news and informed them that by law they would now have to elect a diocesan administrator who would take charge until a new bishop was appointed. They were taken aback by this unexpected announcement.

As I reflected on my seventeen years as bishop of Kamloops, I am so grateful to God for all the good people He sent into my life to share my joys as well as my burdens of office: the priests, the religious women and men; the permanent deacon, Leonard, and his wife Marie; the dedicated staff of the Chancery; the administrators and teachers in our Catholic schools; the many catechists and committee members in our parishes; the young children who brought me so much joy; the St. Vincent de Paul Society; the Knights of Columbus; the Catholic Women's League; the Journey Team; the cordial staff at the Shrine and Retreat House; and so many others who are stored in my memory bank.

There were a few families and friends who accepted me into their homes as a family member, e.g., Gemma Bittante, an exquisite cook and all-around factotum; her husband Arturo, a skilled carpenter, and their three children. The premature and unexpected passing of Arturo brought profound sadness to the family and his many friends.

Then there was my barber and city councillor John DeCicco and his wife Darlene who was also my secretary for five years. I remember John's parents, Lorenzo and Carmela, and his siblings. Lorenzo was so proud that we shared the same name and that I enjoyed his homemade wine. John also made wine but nothing like his father's. We were deeply saddened when Lorenzo passed away. He enjoyed so much playing bocce with us in his back yard after a delicious dinner prepared by Carmela and Darlene. Then there was Joe Stella and the "boys" who would meet at our own "coach's corner" during the intermission at the Kamloops Blazers hockey games in the

Riverside Colosseum. Craig Cook was also a good friend. We shared a common interest—the Chicago Bears football team. He was quite an expert and we would discuss the fate of our beloved team over coffee in good times and in bad. He came to Chicago and was thrilled when I took him to Soldier Field to see a Bears game.

There were so many other people who crossed my path and who made my years in Kamloops so memorable from both a human as well as a spiritual point of view.

The apostles prayed…and laid their hands on them.

(Acts 6:6)

THE "laying on of hands" in our biblical tradition has always been a sign of empowerment and special consecration. The bishop, as successor of the Apostles, has the power to lay hands on those about to be confirmed and on candidates for the Holy Orders of deacon, priest and bishop.

In my more than thirty years as bishop, I had the privilege of administering confirmation to many thousands of candidates. It was always a great joy for me to speak to these young people on this important day in their life.

In the diocese of Kamloops each year on Passion (or Palm) Sunday we had a special program of preparation for the candidates of confirmation. On this weekend we would hold a retreat for the candidates from across the diocese. They usually numbered about three hundred. Those from the remoter outlying parishes would arrive on buses in time for the Friday evening meal followed by the first session. Meals were prepared and served by the various parishes of the city and the sleeping accommodations were provided in parish halls. There was always one adult chaperone for every ten candidates. The diocesan Journey Team took an active role in this preparation program.

On Sunday morning in Our Lady of Perpetual Help Church, I would say the Mass, distribute the palms, and lead the procession with the palms on the church grounds. On Monday morning, all the candidates would assemble in church for the Chrism Mass together with all the priests of the diocese concelebrating the Mass with me. The candidates felt very proud to see their respective pastors present at the Mass. All three oils used in the celebration of the Sacraments were blessed, including the Sacred Chrism. This is the oil that would be used on the day of their confirmation in their parish. This was a very teachable moment. The young people were very happy to be together with so many of their peers at this retreat. After Mass and a quick lunch, they would board their buses to return home after a few hugs with people they had never met before the weekend. This retreat meant that the young people from afar would miss school on the Monday. Their parents felt that the absence was more than justified.

It was also a privilege for me to ordain several transitional deacons. This order constituted them official members of the clergy. A transitional deacon is one who is preparing for the second phase of Holy Orders, which is the priesthood. He is different from a permanent deacon who is usually a married man who does not advance to priesthood.

Another great joy and privilege of a bishop is to ordain men to the priesthood, regardless of age. In my years as bishop, I was privileged to ordain several men as priests, some as diocesan priests and others belonging to religious congregations including Scalabrinians. There is a spiritual bond that develops between a bishop and the priests he ordained. The day that I ordained my first priest as a young auxiliary bishop was a day of extraordinary joy for me because I felt a sense of spiritual fatherhood.

A priest is ordained a bishop by the laying on of hands of the principal consecrator and two co-consecrators. Then all the bishops present also lay hands on the new bishop and embrace him as a brother bishop. On February 2, 1990, it was my privilege to serve as co-consecrator at the episcopal ordination of Bishop Peter Mallon of Nelson, later to become Archbishop of Regina, Saskatchewan.

One of my priorities was to attend the funerals of my diocesan priests and those of my Scalabrinian confreres whenever I could. May God reward them for their priestly and religious service to God's people.

A few days after retiring to Chicago in 1999, I went to pay my respects to Francis Cardinal George. I told him that I would be living in his diocese and felt he should know about it. He welcomed me with open arms as did his vicar general, Bishop Raymond Goedert. The Cardinal asked me about my plans. I told him that I was praying and considering various options. Bad mistake. A few days later he invited me to his home with his vicar general. He said to me: "Do I have an option for you! Please do us a favor and accept to be the pastor of Holy Rosary Church." I'm sure they did some research on me before making me the offer. You can never be too careful!

I thought about it for some time and then said O.K. Holy Rosary Church was only about two miles from where I was born and grew up so it sounded like a good idea. Cardinal George informed me that Holy Rosary was not the Italian national parish it was when I was growing up. It now had a sizable number of Hispanics. I was not unhappy about that at all. I grew up in an immigrant parish and loved the immigrants just like the priests did in my parish of Santa Maria Addolorata. Now it was my turn to do the same. But what about the Spanish language? I decided to go to Mexico for a six-week course of total immersion in Spanish. I had a good tutor. We had three hours of class, six days a week and I studied for four hours each day. That learning experience helped me a lot. It jump-started me on a new and exciting pastoral adventure.

I liked the idea of Holy Rosary Church. The rosary has always been my preferred Marian devotion. I learned how to say it as a boy and have said it every day since. Furthermore, I was consecrated a bishop in Holy Rosary Cathedral in Vancouver and now pastor of Holy Rosary Church in Chicago. I think that the Blessed Virgin Mary was trying to tell me something.

Then the apostles
returned to
their homes.

(Jn 20:10)

AFTER twenty-eight years in Canada, in September of 1999, I returned to Chicago with the feeling of "Home, Sweet Home" in my heart. I hearkened back to the days of my childhood in the Windy City. We were poor but we did not know it. All of our neighbors were also first and second generation immigrants who were in the same condition as we were. But in our poverty, we were very happy because we were able to bond more closely to our parents and siblings. There was no television in those days so we could not compare ourselves with more idyllic families like those in *The Brady Bunch* or *The Waltons* or *Little House on the Prairie*. Our house was the "little apartment in the tenement".

Speaking of tenements, while I was in the minor seminary, we had a very dramatic and enthusiastic English teacher by the name of Fr. Pontarelli. One day in class he said to us: "Hearken and lend me thine ears, o ye fainthearted refugees of the tenements." He did not mean it as a slur. He said it smilingly and with his customary flair, as though he were enacting a scene from Shakespeare. I guess he felt that when we recited poetry, we did so without any emotion. To him it was blah. You should have seen and heard him declaim "to be or not to be". He was a true thespian with a stentorian voice.

Speaking of Shakespeare, there is a story told about a young boy who delivered newspapers every morning. One day a woman met him at the door and complimented him for being so punctual and polite. She asked him his name. He answered "My name is William Shakespeare." She said to him: "My, that is a very famous name." He answered: "It should be: I've been delivering papers in this neighborhood for three years."

When I think of it, I would not have traded my childhood and home life with anyone else's. St. John Vianney once wrote: "The home must be in accord with the Church, that all harmful influences be withheld from the souls of children. Where there is true piety in the home, purity of morals reigns supreme." My parents tried very hard to impart this to us.

Shortly after my arrival in Chicago, on September 8, 1999, I celebrated the fiftieth anniversary of my first religious profession in my home parish of Santa Maria Addolorata. Three Scalabrinian priests from the novitiate class of 1948-1949 joined me: Fr. Angelo Carbone, Fr. Alex Dalpiaz and Fr. John Corrao. The fourth member of our group, Fr. Vincent Monaco, could not join us. The pastor of Santa Maria Addolorata, Fr. Louis Gandolfi, c.s. organized a beautiful liturgy that many Scalabrinian priests, sisters and seminarians attended, along with some friends. All of us were then invited to a luncheon which turned out to be a very entertaining "roast". I could not believe what some of the speakers remembered about the life of the four of us over the last fifty years.

Since I was about to begin a new phase of my life on October 11, I decided to make an eight-day retreat at the Trinity Retreat House in Larchmont, New York. Fr. Benedict Groeschel, Director of the House, was someone I had known from my student days at Iona College. Fr. Benedict is the founder of a new religious community known as the Franciscan Friars of the Renewal. He is a psychologist and was the Director of Spiritual Development for the Archdiocese of New York. He is the author of several books and makes frequent appearances on television station EWTN. My week with him in Larchmont was of great spiritual support for me in this transitional phase of my life.

Later, after completing the aforementioned total immersion course in Spanish in our Scalabrinian seminary in the outskirts of the city of Guadalajara, Mexico, I was ready to check out this Holy Rosary Church. There I met the very likeable pastor, Fr. Anthony Talarico, and his equally likeable Irish wolfhound, appropriately called Muldoon. I checked into Holy Rosary rectory on February 15, 2000, and said my first Mass in the parish the following Sunday. The parishioners welcomed me very cordially but perhaps wondering why their new pastor had to be a bishop. Rumors were circulating that Holy Rosary could be another one of the many parishes destined for closure. Was the bishop sent to give the last rites to the parish? That was certainly not the mandate given me by Cardinal George when he asked me to take Holy Rosary. In any case, I felt much better with the reception given me at Holy Rosary than the one I received in my first parish in North Vancouver, British Columbia.

My formal installation took place on Sunday, June 4. It was quite an unusual ceremony. Usually it is the local episcopal vicar who installs a new pastor. In my case, it was different. The episcopal vicar, Bishop John Manz, was not the only one present for the ceremony.

Seated L-R: Bishop Manz and Bishop Goedert at my installation as pastor.

The vicar general of the archdiocese, Bishop Raymond Goedert, also took part. Two bishops to install a new pastor? I guess the archdiocese was not about to take any chances with me.

Being back in Chicago meant that I could have a closer contact with my relatives and the friends I remembered from my childhood, such as the D'Agostino's: Irene, Lee and Syl. I was pleased to celebrate the fiftieth wedding anniversary of both Lee and Syl and not long afterwards presided at their funeral Masses. Another couple is Gladys and John Nowicki. Both were close to our family and were present at my first Mass in Chicago in 1957. John is a Knight of the Holy Sepulchre.

50th wedding anniversary of cousins Gino and Adelaide Pioli with daughter Germana.

A few months after my installation, I went to Brazil for ten days to visit my relatives, a trip that was planned many months before. I was there to celebrate the fifteith wedding anniversary of my cousins, Gino Pioli and his wife Adelaide in Santo André. I said the Mass in their home and enjoyed a delightful family dinner afterwards. Being in the state of São Paulo, I took the opportunity to visit relatives in Campinas and Rio Claro. Maria Pioli took me to visit the grave of her husband, my dear cousin Nelson. I also called in on the bishop of Santos which is the port city of São Paulo. He is Bishop Jacyr Braido, also a Scalabrinian.

After my sole surviving brother Joe and sister Jenny passed away three weeks apart before Christmas of 2001, I was the last of the immediate Sabatini family. However, my first cousins Ralph and Teresa Rossi are now living in Chicago. They were young children in Valbona during my seminary days in Rome. I would spend a part of my summer vacation with them and we had lots of fun together at that time. Their mother, Aunt Celeste Rossi, my father's sister, often complained to me that I was spending too much time with my other relatives in the Garfagnana. She was to me like a mother in those years I was away from mom and the family.

My cousin Ralph eventually emigrated to Chicago as a teenager in 1956 and in 1970 married Louise Ventura. They have three children. His sister Teresa, who was still in Valbona for my first Mass, followed him to Chicago several years later. She married Joe Calenda in 1979, and they have three daughters.

My Aunt Celeste was very special. She and her husband Domenico owned a cow, a sheep and a goat. My aunt made cheese and cured it with great care. It was the best cheese I ever tasted. She always made sure that I would take back with me to the seminary in Rome a sizeable chunk of her homemade cheese. So my Aunt Celeste was the cheese maker and my Uncle Decimo was the wine maker. Quite a delightful combination!

In the year 2003, Aunt Celeste was ninety-three years old and in failing health. Ralph, Teresa and I decided to go to Italy visit her. She suffered from senility and was in and out of consciousness. Before I entered her room to see her, her daughter-in-law Rosemary, who cared for her with such love, told me that she would probably not recognize me. She told me that Aunt Celeste was not very lucid and did not recognize many people. When I went in to see her and told her who I was, immediately she opened her eyes and looked at me. Rosemary tried to test her and asked: "Do you know who this is?" Showing some annoyance, she answered: "Of course I do. It's my nephew Padre Renzo", as she always called me. Before leaving Valbona, I gave her Holy Viaticum. She died a short time afterwards. Her death was a great loss to the Rossi family and to me.

In the summer of 1999, just a few months before my retirement, cousins Ralph and Louise came to spend their vacation with me in Kamloops. We had such a good time together. I took them to visit Vancouver, Whistler, Vancouver Island, and many other beautiful places in British Columbia.

Cousins Ralph and Louise Rossi and Butchart Gardens on Vancouver Island.

On September 3, 2003, Ralph and Louise's youngest daughter Amanda married Daniel Donato. At their request, I was so pleased to perform the wedding in Holy Rosary Church. On December 17, 2007,

I was delighted to baptize their first child. I was thrilled when they gave the baby girl the name Gianna. It reminded me of what took place in October of 1997 at the second World Meeting of Families in Rio de Janeiro. A young woman stepped forward to address the crowd gathered around Pope John Paul II at the Maracanà Stadium. She gave a moving testimony and then offered this prayer: "Dear Mama: Thank you for having given me life two times: when you conceived me and when you permitted me to be born, protecting my life. My life seeks to be the natural continuation of your life, of your joy of living, your enthusiasm. . . Dear Mama, intercede always for all mothers and all families who turn to you and entrust themselves to you." The pope was visibly moved as he listened to this woman named Gianna Emanuela Molla. The Pope knew Gianna's mother well. Her name was Gianna Beretta Molla. She was a physician who was not afraid to use her position to testify to her belief in the sacredness of every human life. When she was pregnant with Gianna, she was discovered to have fibroma. The doctors told her that the only way they could save her life was to abort the baby. This either-or dilemma no longer exists due to advances in medical technology. In any case, for Gianna, direct abortion was not an option. She was ready to die rather than to destroy her child's life. She told the doctor: "I am ready for anything as long as my baby is saved." The baby Gianna Emanuela was saved but her mother was not.

On April 24, 1994, three years before the meeting in Brazil, Pope John Paul II had beatified Gianna Beretta Molla, calling her "a woman of heroic love". Present at the beatification were her husband, her brothers and sisters, and her three surviving children, including Gianna Emanuela. It was Mother's Day in Brazil.

For all eight years that I was pastor of Holy Rosary, I had the companionship of Fr. Bill Woestman, O.M.I. Fr. Bill and I were students at the Gregorian University in Rome for six years. We graduated from the School of Philosophy in 1953 and Theology in 1957, the year of our ordination. Our paths separated after that, until he came to live at Holy Rosary a few months after I arrived. We had eight wonderful years together. Fr. Bill is a professional canon lawyer and has written several books on the subject of church law. During the week he worked in the archdiocesan tribunal. On weekends he helped me with the Masses.

What was the life of pastor at Holy Rosary like? In the immortal words of Forrest Gump's Momma: "Life was like a box of chocolates. You never know what you're gonna get." The chocolates

Top: "Where's Waldo"—middle left somewhere. Fr. Bill Woestman, O.M.I. top row, 4th from right.

Center: 80th birthday of Lenora Phillips (in wheelchair) and group of friends in parish garden.

Left: "Taste of Holy Rosary" with Ron Lenzi, L, and Sam Natale, R.

I received at Holy Rosary were very much to my liking. The parishioners were very cooperative and easy to work with. The multicultural composition of the parish added a richness to the faith community. In the years I was there, the Anglos and the Hispanics worked very well together (photograph, p. 159). They were able to accomplish many worthwhile projects. They held an annual banquet at which they honored some deserving parishioners. They organized annual affairs called "the Taste of Holy Rosary," "A Day at the Races" and "Riverfest". I enjoyed working with people such as Danny Serrelli, Ron Lenzi and son Ron, Tony Langone, Barbara Meccia, Frank Nocita, Reyna Luna, Adeline Chapel (a great baker) and her sister Connie Griff (who provided me with pretzels for the football games), Mike and Tina DiCapua (whom I married), Ida DiPrima (who made the best fried zucchini flowers), and others whose names I may have forgotten. The parishioners also cooperated with every initiative designed to improve the spiritual and devotional life of the community. Among the leaders on these efforts were Marge Ruffalo, Marie Parillo, Dolly Donatelle, Josephine Tenuto, and many others. Coming from ministry in a huge missionary diocese, the life of pastor at Holy Rosary was a piece of cake (or box of chocolates). The people made life easy for me, out of respect for my age, perhaps?

"Riverfest": L-R, Fr. Vincent Gennardo, c.s., Fr. Dan LaPolla, c.s. (my deacon) and Roz Cangelosi.

Catechism teachers: standing L-R, Marie Palese, D.R.E.; Clair Zaffaroni, Deanna Kozak, Debbie Kozak, Jim Campion; seated, Connie McCartney, Jack McCartney, Stephanie Rivera, Angelo Paone, Pastor Fr. Michael Kalck. (absent, Jackie Pacione)

Above: Staff members Pat Bragagnolo, L, and Linda Keaty, R.

Left: Bob Luby—"Mr. Fixit" and "Mr. Coffee".

My life as a pastor at Holy Rosary was a real blessing for me. First of all I must acknowledge the warm reception I received from His Eminence Cardinal George and all the active and retired auxiliary bishops of Chicago. They all welcomed me with open arms. This was a source of great encouragement to me.

Sometimes Cardinal George invited me to his home for dinner with his auxiliary bishops and the other bishops living in Chicago. It was so good to be together with the Cardinal and brother bishops in such an informal and joyful setting.

Knowing how Cardinal George and bishops treated me, my "cousins" Ron Lenzi, his wife Gerry Michelotti, and their three sons, Ron Jr., E.J., and Larry, hosted an annual Christmas dinner for the cardinal and the bishops in a private room of their Erie Café. It was a lot of fun and served to enhance the spirit of Christmas. After I retired as pastor, one of the bishops asked me if my retirement marked the end of our annual Christmas dinner at the Erie. I mentioned this to Ron and he said: "Absolutely not. It's business as usual."

The parishioners of Holy Rosary were equally good to me and able to put up with my quirks and idiosyncrasies. Especially empathetic towards me were the parish secretary Pat Bragagnolo, caretaker Bob Luby, and all-around man Jim Campion. They even politely endured my corny jokes. Deacon Jorge Rozo and wife Nubia helped to hold the Latino community together. They were helped by Irene Soto, her husband Francisco, daughter Laura Flores and her husband Ruben. All of these put up with my limited Spanish.

Then there were all those generous people of both language groups who volunteered their services in every aspect of parish life: the finance committee; those who prepared and took part in the liturgy of the Mass—lectors, commentators, Eucharistic ministers, altar servers, ushers; those who cleaned the altar linens; those who volunteered to teach the Liturgy of the Word for children at Sunday Mass and regular catechism classes after Mass; the church musicians and choirs; and so many others to

English Choir: top, Bob Palese and Lucy Parzyszek; bottom, Leticia Gallardo, Alma Bragagnolo, and organist Alberta Catalano. (absent: Mike Seiberlich, associate organist)

Spanish Choir: L-R, Yolanda Gutierrez, Silvia León, Laura Flores, Stephanie Rojas, Jonathan Flores, Oracio Bahena, Oscar Tobon, Jesús Bahena. (absent: Fernando Roman)

whom I will be forever grateful, like the weekday morning Mass crowd, my faithful master of ceremonies Steven Zaffaroni, and assistant sacristans Sally Greco and Roseann Cacioppo.

One of our faithful altar servers was Joe Mendoza. He was always there when you needed him, and he taught the new recruits how to serve. One day his Aunt Pat asked him who were the two people he admired most. He answered: "Bishop Sabatini and Al Capone.' Did he notice some similarity?

In September of 2003, I celebrated the twenty-fifth anniversary of my consecration as bishop. On September 18, I concelebrated Mass with a number of Scalabrinian priests from both the Chicago and New York Provinces. On the following Sunday, September 21, the exact date of my consecration, I said the Jubilee Mass for the parishioners of Holy Rosary.

Somewhat the same arrangement took place in March 2007 for the fiftieth anniversary of my ordination as a priest. The anniversary Mass took place on Sunday, March 18, in Holy Rosary with Cardinal George present. The annual awards banquet took place after the Mass.

This was part one of the celebration.

The second part took place the following evening, March 19, the actual date of my ordination. A second jubilee Mass was celebrated with numerous Scalabrinian priests, sisters, seminarians and parishioners. This was followed by a dinner for our religious communities at the Erie Café. Since my return to Chicago, Ron and Gerry and their family have been very good to me and to the parishioners of Holy Rosary.

In the meantime, my relatives in Italy were pleading with me to go to Valbona to celebrate also with them the twenty-fifth anniversary of my ordination as bishop. They remembered that I had gone there twenty-five years before to celebrate Mass as a new bishop. So on October 24, 2003, I went to Italy and said Mass in the church of Valbona on Sunday, October 26. We had another family dinner afterwards with thirty-five of my close relatives present.

Of course, now my relatives in Brazil were a bit jealous. They wanted a piece of the action. I accommodated them by going to Brazil in January of 2004. Again it was a very warm reunion. I also had occasion to visit the new Scalabrinian seminary in Paraguay.

PREVIOUS PAGE
Top: 25th Anniversary Mass of episcopal ordination with Scalabrinian confreres.

Center: Cardinal George speaking at my 50th anniversary of priestly ordination: L-R, flanked by Deacon Jorge Rozo and Master of Ceremonies Steven Zaffaroni; in back, Fr. Woestman and Fr. Dan Flens.

Bottom: Anniversary banquet: seated L-R, Fr. Vincent Monaco, c.s., Fr. Edward Moretti, Cardinal George, Fr. Woestman; standing, Fr. Gino Dalpiaz, c.s., Fr. Dan Flens, Fr. Valente, Fr. Charles Zanoni, c.s., Fr. Szabelski, and former pastor Fr. Anthony Talarico.

THIS PAGE
Second Jubilee Mass.

The year 2004 was a banner year for Holy Rosary Parish. It marked the centennial of the foundation of the parish. The episcopal vicar, Bishop John Manz, celebrated the anniversary Mass on Saturday, July 10. The church was filled with present and former parishioners. The Jubilee Committee had worked very hard to prepare this historic event. The streets of the parish were decorated with banners. A commemorative booklet was published with photographs of parish families. Later, on July 31, Bishop Manz returned to bless the newly renovated parish center.

The year 2005 was another milestone in the history of the Scalabrinian family. It marked the centennial of the death of the founder. Celebrations were held on June 1 in all areas of the Scalabrinian world. The main celebration, however, was held at the Motherhouse in Piacenza, Italy. I was privileged to be there for that historic moment, together with the other Scalabrinian bishops, priests, sisters and a large crowd of the faithful. The Solemn Mass took place in the Cathedral of Piacenza where the body of Blessed John Baptist Scalabrini is buried.

I planned to be in Italy a few days before the celebration so as to visit some of my relatives. It was on this occasion that I visited my ailing Uncle Decimo and Aunt Anna in Valbona.

I gave them both the Anointing of the Sick in the paternal home of the Sabatinis in Valbona. After my uncle retired, he and his wife Anna had gone to live there. My uncle led a very exemplary life. As long as he was able, he went to Mass every morning and did plenty of spiritual reading. He often walked to the cemetery to visit the graves of his parents and siblings, including my father. Uncle Decimo never knew his mother. She died giving birth to him. Hence, he was given the name Decimo which means the tenth child.

When I visited my aunt and uncle on that day in 2005, we knew that this could very well be the last time we would meet on this earth. So we spent the time talking and reminiscing about days gone by when I would visit them as a seminarian. In their earlier years, Uncle Decimo and his family lived for years on a farm where he raised a pig, a cow, a mule, chickens and rabbits. He made his own salami, prosciutto and sausages. My aunt Anna made the chicken soup and all the pasta for the tortellini and ravioli. She was a great cook. In addition to looking after the farm and the vineyard, uncle Decimo also cared for his older brother Giuseppe who lived with them. He had a very severe case of Parkinson's disease and could not look after himself for years. Uncle Giuseppe was a kindly person who was very proud of me. Unfortunately, he died one year before my ordination as a priest. With uncle and aunt we talked about many things including the fig tree in front of their farmhouse. Unlike the fig tree in Jesus' story, this one produced very good fruit. I enjoyed plucking the figs from the tree and eating those succulent delicacies. I had never tasted any like them before nor ever since.

We talked about Uncle Decimo's mule named Storna. I was a bit embarrassed in my visits when my uncle insisted that I ride the mule to Valbona while he walked in front. My uncle was so proud when he was asked to take the local bishop on his mule to Valbona for confirmation of the children. Once he even gave a ride on his mule to the President of Italy. My uncle kept a picture of Storna on the wall of his house.

This last visit to Uncle Decimo and Aunt Anna in 2005 marked the end of a very loving phase of my life. Both of them passed away in their nineties a few months apart not long after my visit.

As I think back, I was so happy to have been in Valbona in 1992 to celebrate Uncle Decimo and Aunt Anna's fiftieth wedding anniversary. On May 31, 2005, on the eve of the celebration in Piacenza, I went to the town of Durlo, high upon a mountain in the Veneto region of Italy for the funeral of Scalabrinian bishop Marco Caliaro. During my six years as a seminarian in Rome, Fr. Caliaro was my confessor and spiritual director. He had a very positive influence in my formation. As a priest, he was the master of ceremonies of Cardinal Piazza at my ordination to the priesthood. Some years later he was named bishop of Sabina and Poggio Mirteto, outside of Rome. He was the second Scalabrinian to be named bishop. The first was Bishop Massimo Rinaldi, whose cause for beatification is in process in Rome. Bishop Caliaro was overjoyed when I was named the third bishop in our community. We kept in close contact and I visited him on occasion after he retired to the Shrine of the Blessed Virgin in Rivergaro. Bishop Caliaro was present in Rome with all the Scalabrinian bishops for the beatification of the founder. He was somewhat instrumental in

50th wedding anniversary of Decimo and Anna Sabatini, together with the pastor of Valbona, Fr. Giovanni Giannotti.

bringing this about. He had collaborated with another Scalabrinian, Fr. Mario Francesconi, in writing a very comprehensive and well-researched biography of Bishop Scalabrini. It is significant that Bishop Caliaro should pass away on the eve of the centennial of the death of the founder whom he loved and admired.

In June of 2007 a former student of mine, Fr. John Meneghetti, c.s. invited me to administer two confirmations in his parish in Bedford, England, on my way to Italy. I accepted because of our long-time association. Fr. John was very cordial to me as he was when I visited him on several occasions in Milan. He was then pastor of the beautiful Church of La Madonna del Carmine. As pastor in Milan, Fr. John was very kind to my Novice Master Fr. Ansaldi, who lived with him for several years. I thanked him for that.

During my short stay, Fr. John drove me to visit the famous Cambridge University and King's College. The martyred English cardinal, St. John Fisher, was ordained in Cambridge at the age of twenty-two and became chancellor of the university in 1501. King Henry VIII had him beheaded in 1549 for refusing to sign his Act of Supremacy. St. John Fisher was the victim of King Henry's break with the Roman Catholic Church.

Fr. John also took me to visit the American Cemetery and World War II memorial in Cambridge. The chapel of the cemetery had a huge map on the wall displaying all of the European military campaigns during the war including where my brother Ralph had fought. The cemetery was absolutely first class, with the hundreds of marble Crosses and Stars of David marking the graves of our fallen soldiers.

Afterwards I made my way to Tuscany to celebrate my fiftieth anniversary as priest with my relatives in the Garfagnana. The town of Castiglione where several of my relatives lived organized a special feast for my anniversary. It took place in the parish church on Sunday, June 10, 2007, the feast of Corpus Christi. After the Solemn Mass, I carried the Blessed Sacrament through the streets of the town accompanied by the town band. After the procession, the acting mayor and town council members (one of whom was a cousin of mine) held a reception for me in the town hall. Much to my surprise, they made me an honorary citizen of the town that was so well known to my parents.

Then it was on to Valbona (now by car) for the anniversary Mass in the parish church. After Mass, the usual dinner for family and friends took place under a tent in the small town square. The Scalabrinian vicar general, Fr. Livio Stella (my associate in North Vancouver in the 70's) came from Rome for the occasion together with Fr. Agostino Lovatin, c.s.

During my brief stay in Valbona one of my treasured visits was to the little cemetery where I had celebrated an outdoor memorial Mass on October 1, 1998, on the fiftieth anniversary of my father's death. This time it was important for me to pay my respects also to all my deceased uncles and aunts, especially my Uncle Decimo and Aunt Anna and Aunt Celeste, who had passed away before this visit.

Banquet after Jubilee Mass: L-R, cousins Antonietta and Carmen, Fr. Livio Stella, c.s., Fr. Agostino Lovatin, c.s., and to my left, Isabel Palazzo.

According to the code of canon law, when a pastor reaches the age of seventy-five, he must hand in his resignation to his diocesan bishop. When in 2005 I turned seventy-five, I sent my letter to Cardinal George. It must have gotten lost in the mail. I never received a written answer. Some time later when I met the Cardinal, he said to me with a smile on his face: "Larry, you're not going anywhere." I guess he wanted to give me a little more time to redeem myself. Finally, three years later, I had to bring up the subject again and told the cardinal that I felt unable to continue as pastor. This time he accepted my resignation. Then, the whole process of naming a new pastor began and a successor was eventually appointed. He is Fr. Michael Kalck, a diocesan priest who taught Latin and Greek in Quigley Seminary for several years. He accepted his first appointment as pastor with great energy and enthusiasm. He said that being assigned to Holy Rosary was like winning the lottery. He was right.

On Sunday, September 7, 2008, Bishop John Manz, episcopal vicar, came to Holy Rosary for the formal installation of the new pastor (photograph, p. 159). In his address to the congregation, he thanked me for my years of service and suggested that the parish dedicate the new parking lot in my name. I said to him: "Thanks but no thanks. When you have a washroom on an Indian reservation in Western Canada named after you, that's as good as it gets. Any additional dedication would be a letdown."

Since retirement I said Mass a few times for some football teams. I was invited by the Syracuse University football team to say

Mass for them in the hotel in Chicago prior to their game against Northwestern. I said the Mass, gave them a pep talk, and wished them well. They lost the game by a wide margin. Scalabrinian Father Nick Marro, pastor of St. Lucy Church, has been chaplain of the Chicago Bears since before they won the Super Bowl in 1985. He invited me to say Mass in the hotel for the Bears a few times. Every time I said the Mass, I was given a bench pass and stood behind the players' bench hoping and praying. But each time the Bears lost the game. With my track record, I don't suppose I will be getting any more invitations.

However, there were happier moments also. September 21 was the thirtieth anniversary of my ordination as bishop. I celebrated Mass in Holy Rosary on that day and another Mass the following evening for the Scalabrinian priests, sisters and seminarians in the Chicago area.

Now as a man of "leisure", I decided, after nine years, to take a trip to Vancouver and Kamloops where I spent twenty-eight years of my life. I was there from October 3–14, 2008. My trip took me first to St. Stephen's Church in North Vancouver for Mass and reception on Sunday, October 5. It brought back so many memories of my first parish. I met several parishioners who were there in the 70's: Renée Stark and her niece Nicole, Jack and Mavis Toovey and many others. I also visited the Scalabrinian parishes of Our Lady of Sorrows and St. Helen's. My driver was Fr. Pat Teeporten. He took me to visit Holy Rosary Cathedral where I was consecrated a bishop and met the new Archbishop Michael Moore. I could not believe how much Vancouver changed; at the time, it was making huge preparations for the forthcoming Olympics.

We also visited the churches of Holy Name and Holy Cross in Burnaby where I had been pastor. Fr. Pat had been my associate at Holy Name, and a good companion.

From there it was on to Kamloops for an emotional visit. I was invited to stay at Our Lady of Perpetual Help where the pastor was Fr. Peter Nguyen. He was a Vietnamese boat person whom the diocese sponsored from a refugee camp in the Philippines. After he came, he continued his studies in the seminary in Vancouver. I had ordained him a priest for the Diocese of Kamloops eighteen years ago. I said Mass for the parishioners as well as the schoolchildren whom I also visited in their classrooms. I had lunch with the school principal and staff, most of whom were teaching there when I was their bishop. I visited my successor, Bishop David Monroe, and the Chancery Office staff, most of whom were also there during my tenure. While in Kamloops,

I arranged to visit the graves of Msgr. MacIntyre, my vicar general for seventeen years, and my friend Fr. Ray McLeod.

Of course, I had to make a visit to my pride and joy—the Shrine of the Immaculate Heart of Mary in Cache Creek.

Monday, October 13, was Canadian Thanksgiving Day. I celebrated Mass for the Carmelite Sisters in Armstrong and visited with them for a while as we used to do. That evening I had Thanksgiving dinner in a new restaurant on the St. Joseph's Indian reservation with my successor, the very capable Bishop David Monroe, Fr. Nguyen, Mrs. Gemma Bittante who had been my homemaker for many years, and her three daughters.

The following day I was back home in Chicago reliving the joy of the visit.

While driving in the streets of Chicago and suburbs, I often had to stop at railroad crossings, and I would watch the freight trains go by. Some of them were carrying lumber from the diocese of Kamloops. In the diocese we had five large sawmills. The lumber on the train is covered with plastic bearing the logo of the company. I saw names like West Fraser, from the sawmill in Quesnel; Canoe, from the sawmill in Armstrong; and Talko, from the large sawmill just outside of Kamloops. Watching the railroad cars go by reminded me of the beautiful years I spent there as a missionary bishop.

Retired life does provide an opportunity to continue doing some pastoral work insofar as one's health will allow. Some of my religious confreres took advantage of this. Two of my former theology students are now pastors in Rhode Island. Fr. Charles Zanoni, c.s. is pastor of St. Rocco's Church and Fr. Alfred Almonte, c.s. is pastor of St. Bartholomew's Church. The two of them "plotted" together and invited me to preach a Lenten mission in their parishes. The first mission was at St. Rocco's from March 28 till April 4, 2009, while the second was at St. Bartholomew's during Holy Week from Palm Sunday to Easter Sunday. I enjoyed my stay there and had a chance to meet with some Scalabrinian religious from the Providence and Boston areas—people I had not seen for many years. This included Bro. Lou Callisto, c.s. and Fr. Ed Marino, c.s., director of the award-winning Villa Scalabrini in North Kingstown. This is the villa where my classmate and friend Fr. Monaco, c.s. passed away less than a year before. I was able to spend Easter Sunday with my New York friends John and Terry Valitutto in the city of Newport, Rhode Island.

This is as far as my journey has taken me. As I look back it was quite a diversified experience. I was involved in many different forms of ministry. This prompted one of my friends to say to me: "What's wrong with you? Could you not hold down one job?" No matter what the task at hand was, I was very happy doing it, because I felt that this is what God in His divine wisdom was asking me to do.

I never regretted my response to the call of God. Someone once asked me if I had a chance would I do it all over again?

My answer was a definite "yes".

Epilogue

AT nineteen years of age, when I was preparing to make my vows of poverty, chastity and obedience, I had the same concern that Peter and the apostles had when they decided to follow Jesus. Peter said to the Lord: "Look, we have left everything and followed you. What then will we have?" They were very concerned about their future security. Jesus said to them: "Truly I tell you…everyone who has left houses or brothers or sisters or father or mother or children or fields for my sake will receive a hundredfold, and will inherit eternal life." (Mt. 19: 27, 29). Now sixty years later, I can truthfully say that the Lord has kept His promise. As you have read, my journey was blessed with far more than a hundredfold. The Lord was much more generous than what He had promised. I left something behind and I found much more than I left, including a sense of joy and fulfillment in doing God's bidding. I appreciate the words of Meister Eckhart, O.P., German theologian and mystic of the thirteenth and fourteenth century who wrote: "Be prepared at all times for the gifts of God and be ready always for new ones. For God is a thousand times more ready to give than we are to receive."

Now I am continuing to work on the second promise that Jesus made to his apostles, namely, eternal life. Achieving this is a lifelong task. It requires a genuine commitment to live out every day the gift of faith that the Lord has given us. My role model, St. Augustine, in a discourse on the Psalms, wrote: "Our thoughts in this present life should turn to the praise of God, because it is in praising God that we shall rejoice forever in the life to come, and no one can be ready for the next life unless he trains himself for it now."

It saddens me to know that there are people in the world with no faith and no belief in God or the love shown us by Christ who died for our salvation. There are those who profess that there is no God, that God is dead, or that God is not great. They have no idea what they are missing. I pray for them often just as the Universal Church prays for them in the Liturgy of the Lord's Passion on Good Friday: "Let us pray for those who do not believe in God, that they may find Him by sincerely following all that is right."

May we all one day join hands and sing together that popular hymn by Carl Boberg with words by Stuart K. Hine:

> When Christ shall come with shout of acclamation,
> And take me home, what joy shall fill my heart!
> Then I shall bow in humble adoration
> And there proclaim, my God, how great Thou art!

In the Bible, the words of St. Paul to Timothy are encouraging:

> "I have fought the good fight, I have finished the race, I have kept the faith. From now on there is reserved for me the crown of righteousness, which the Lord, the righteous judge, will give me on that day, and not only to me but also to all who have longed for His appearing." *(2 Tim. 4:7-8)*

As I continue the last leg of my journey, the thought of that crown is what impels me. May your journey be filled with much love, peace and happiness.

Appendix One

Official Convocation of the Synod of the Diocese of Kamloops (Journey in Faith)

Sacred Heart Cathedral
December 22, 1991

Dear Friends in Christ,

Today marks the 46th anniversary of the founding of the Kamloops Diocese. During these many years, several events took place which changed the course of human history as well as the life of the Church in our Diocese and around the world. Most recently, the dismantling of the once powerful Communist empire gives hope of religious freedom to communities of believers previously oppressed and in some cases openly persecuted.

In the mid-sixties during a time of huge moral upheaval in the world, the Church, under the guidance of the Holy Spirit, concluded an ecumenical council known to history as the Second Vatican Council. The 16 published documents of this council called for a renewal of the universal Church in all of its aspects both spiritual and temporal.

In 1984 our present Holy Father, John Paul II, made an historic pastoral visit to Canada. In his numerous addresses to the Canadian people he called for a renewed commitment to the teachings and principles of the Second Vatican Council. Now, twenty-five years after the conclusion of the Council, we must examine ourselves individually and as Church, on how we have integrated the Council teachings and how well we have implemented them in all areas of life.

Today we formally initiate a process to help us in this self-discovery. It is called a Diocesan Synod. The Synod is a journey we take together. It is a Journey in Faith. We cannot overlook the fact that since the Second Vatican Council, different opinions and different perspectives have surfaced in the Church and in the world. Good people who love the Lord and love the Church which is His Body, have formulated different ideas about what it means to be Church and the course of action which the Church must pursue today and in the future. We cannot afford to let these differences become so rigid and so polarized that we are no longer one Church together. This is why we must seek the guidance of the Holy Spirit who is the interior source of life and movement in the Church. It is the Holy Spirit who will allow us to experience that unity which Jesus wants for the whole Church.

I am convoking this first-ever Synod in the Diocese of Kamloops because I want all the people of our Diocese—young and old, sick and disabled, clergy, religious, laity—to experience with me the great potential that exists among us. We are men and women of faith but we must journey together towards a deeper faith. We all have our own unique assortment of gifts and talents but when these are joined with the gifts of the Holy Spirit, which we have all received in Baptism and Confirmation, then we can do amazing things together. We can experience the joy of being Church together and we can achieve a remarkable sense of unity.

My task as Bishop in this process will be to listen to you and to pray for you that you will be open to the guidance of the Holy Spirit. Each and every one of you must recognize how important his or her views or insights will be to this Synodal process.

It is our general plan to conclude the Diocesan Synod in 1995 the 50th anniversary of the foundation of the Kamloops Diocese. In these intervening years our goal will be to review together our commitment as Church as well as our priorities. But above all, we should seek to energize ourselves spiritually as the People of God. To achieve this we must become People of Prayer. Prayer is the goal of all our activities because prayer means union with God which is the reason for the Church's existence and the goal of all human life and activity. It is in prayer that we express the supremacy of God in all things. It is in prayer that we find the root of our social action on behalf of our needy brothers and sisters. All social consciousness is nurtured and evaluated in prayer.

I ask you then, my brothers and sisters, to pray with me every day for the success of our Diocesan Synod. Our present Holy Father once stated: "We realize more profoundly now since the Council, that in every local church (diocese) gathered in prayer around its bishop there dwells the incomparable beauty of the whole Catholic Church as the faithful image of the praying Christ." (June 1988)

On this fourth Sunday of Advent, our thoughts turn to Mary who gave birth to the Christ Child, the Saviour of the world. The Immaculate Heart of Mary is the principal patroness of the Diocese of Kamloops. We place ourselves under her maternal mantle of love as we walk together in the Journey in Faith. May the Holy Spirit guide us in charting a course towards the year 2000 for ourselves as the Church of the Kamloops Diocese and as part of the One, Holy, Catholic, Apostolic Church.

And now it is my singular privilege to convoke a Synod for the Diocese of Kamloops on this 22nd day of December 1991, 46th anniversary of the Kamloops Diocese.

Most Rev. Lawrence Sabatini, CS
Bishop of Kamloops

NOTE: On October 22–26, 1995, the formal Synod with its forty delegates from across the diocese took place in the Shrine of the Immaculate Heart of Mary in Cache Creek. On January 12, 1996, a forty-page Post-Synodal Letter entitled "Our Journey in Faith—A Vision for the Year 2000" was published by the Bishop. It contained a summary and comments on the pastoral statements developed by the Synod Commissions and the sixty-seven recommendations of the synodal delegates. These centered around five major themes: liturgy, Christian education of children, youth and adults, social justice, and governance and administration.

Appendix Two

Example of a Mini-Pastoral Letter

Second Sunday of Easter
April, 1999

> Jesus said to (Thomas), 'Have you believed because you have seen me? Blessed are those who have not seen and yet have come to believe.' *(John 20:29)*

Dearly beloved in Christ,

These words of Jesus in today's gospel seem very encouraging because they apply to each one of us who has come to believe in the Risen Lord without the benefit of human experience. Yet, the thought has often occurred to me that perhaps my faith today would be so much stronger had I had the good fortune of living during the time of Christ: to hear His voice, to see His smile, to witness His love for children, to observe even just one of His many miracles, perhaps even to eat with Him.

Nonetheless, today's gospel only served to shatter my impossible dream. After all, the Apostles did in fact experience everything I dreamed of. They lived closely to Jesus and yet found it so difficult to believe in Him, especially at crunch time. Let's look at some hard cold facts:

Peter. This is the man who once said to Jesus: "though all become deserters because of you, I will never desert you" (Matthew 25:33). This is the Peter who in a momentary display of courage cuts off the ear of Malchus in the Garden of Olives. Yet, only a few hours later, in the courtyard of Pilate, all the bravado is gone and he denies three times that he ever knew Jesus.

Judas. This is the one who was hand-picked by Jesus and appointed treasurer of the band of apostles. But the lure of money got the better of him. For thirty pieces of power and security, he betrayed the Lord.

The disciples on the road to Emmaus. These two were strong believers in Jesus. But they were crushed and demoralized by the tragic events of Good Friday. For them it was all over. Their hopes had been shattered. Even when the women told them about the empty tomb on Easter morning, they dismissed it as idle gossip. The Risen Lord walked with them along the way and they had difficulty recognizing Him.

The other Apostles. These were the men who had argued about who would hold the top positions in the new kingdom. After the death of Jesus, they were holed up in a secret hideaway, scared to death that any day they too might be arrested and punished for their association with a convicted criminal.

Thomas. This is the protagonist in today's gospel. Initially he appeared to be distrustful and unbelieving. He did not feel like fraternizing with those who remained loyal to a dead leader and a shattered organization.

There are two aspects to St, Thomas' momentary lapse:

Thomas withdrew from the community of believers in a time of great need. All the apostles were hurting but they stayed together. Thomas decided to go it alone—and as a result he missed out on the first visit of the Risen Lord.

Are there not times when we too experience a crisis of faith and feel like leaving the Church? We may even be able to come up with some apparent good reasons. But Christ reaches out and touches our lives through the community which is the Church. If we are not there every Sunday to celebrate the Resurrection of Christ, we too will miss out on the riches of God's grace. Dietrich Bonhoeffer is a Christian martyr who wrote about life in a Nazi concentration camp. He said that his greatest hunger was not for food but for being with his Christian brothers and sisters. We need to remain faithful to the Church community no matter how severe our doubts or perplexities might be. If we leave the Church, we are left with our confused thoughts and will miss the resurrection gift we need most. It is the Church community which supports and strengthens us when our faith is weak. We in turn support and strengthen others when their faith is weak.

Thomas demanded the gift of Resurrection life on his own terms. He would believe only if he could see Christ's wounds and touch them. Thomas laid down the terms and conditions under which God had to act. Somehow we can sympathize with Thomas, because we live in a scientific age which demands scientific proof for everything. It was a case of "I'm from Missouri; show me."

Almost a century ago, an old man was travelling alone in France by train. Seated next to him on the train was a much younger man who kept eyeing the old man as he reached into his travelling case, took out a Bible, and began to read. After a while, the younger man decided to strike up a conversation. "What are you reading?" he asked. The old man answered, "I'm reading from the Bible—the New Testament—the sixth chapter of St. Mark's gospel." The younger man asked: "What does it say?" And the old man said: "It's the story of the miracle of the loaves and fishes. The Gospel writer is saying that a large crowd of people had followed Jesus because of the signs he was performing for the sick. Jesus had preached to the crowd until it was dark and the people were hungry. With only five barley loaves and a couple of dried fishes Jesus fed the entire crowd of 5,000 people. And when the people had finished eating, they filled twelve baskets with the leftovers." The younger man then said quite scornfully: "You don't really believe that stuff, do you?" And the older man said: "Indeed I do." And the younger man then said with an air of disdain: "I can see that you have been brainwashed by ancient superstitions. That could never happen to me. You see, I am a scientist. Everything that happens in this world can ultimately be accounted for scientifically. The story you just read defies the laws of science and therefore is sheer fantasy. Give me facts, provable facts. As a man of science, I can have no faith in miracles. But I cannot expect someone like you to understand that."

At this point in the conversation the train began to slow down. The younger man said, "This is my station," and as he rose from his seat, he said to the older man: "It was nice talking with you, Mr. ... I'm sorry, I didn't get your name." The older man handed him his calling card which bore the name "Louis Pasteur"—one of the world's great scientists.

Faith and science are not at war with one another. Science becomes a problem only when it makes itself into a god and uses technology as the last word. Pope John Paul II points this out in his recent encyclical titled Faith and Reason.

Today's gospel has a happy ending. Thomas is able to set aside his doubts and make an inspiring profession of faith: "My Lord and my God." He then lived it to the point of a martyr's death. May we show forth that same kind of faith in our daily lives.

With kindest personal regards and my prayers for the Lord's blessings on you and your loved ones, I am

Devotedly yours in Christ,

Most Rev. Lawrence Sabatini, CS
Bishop of Kamloops

Index

(*Italics* indicate a photograph)